AF411205
PLEASE
LEAVE ALL
BAGS AT
FRONT
COUNT

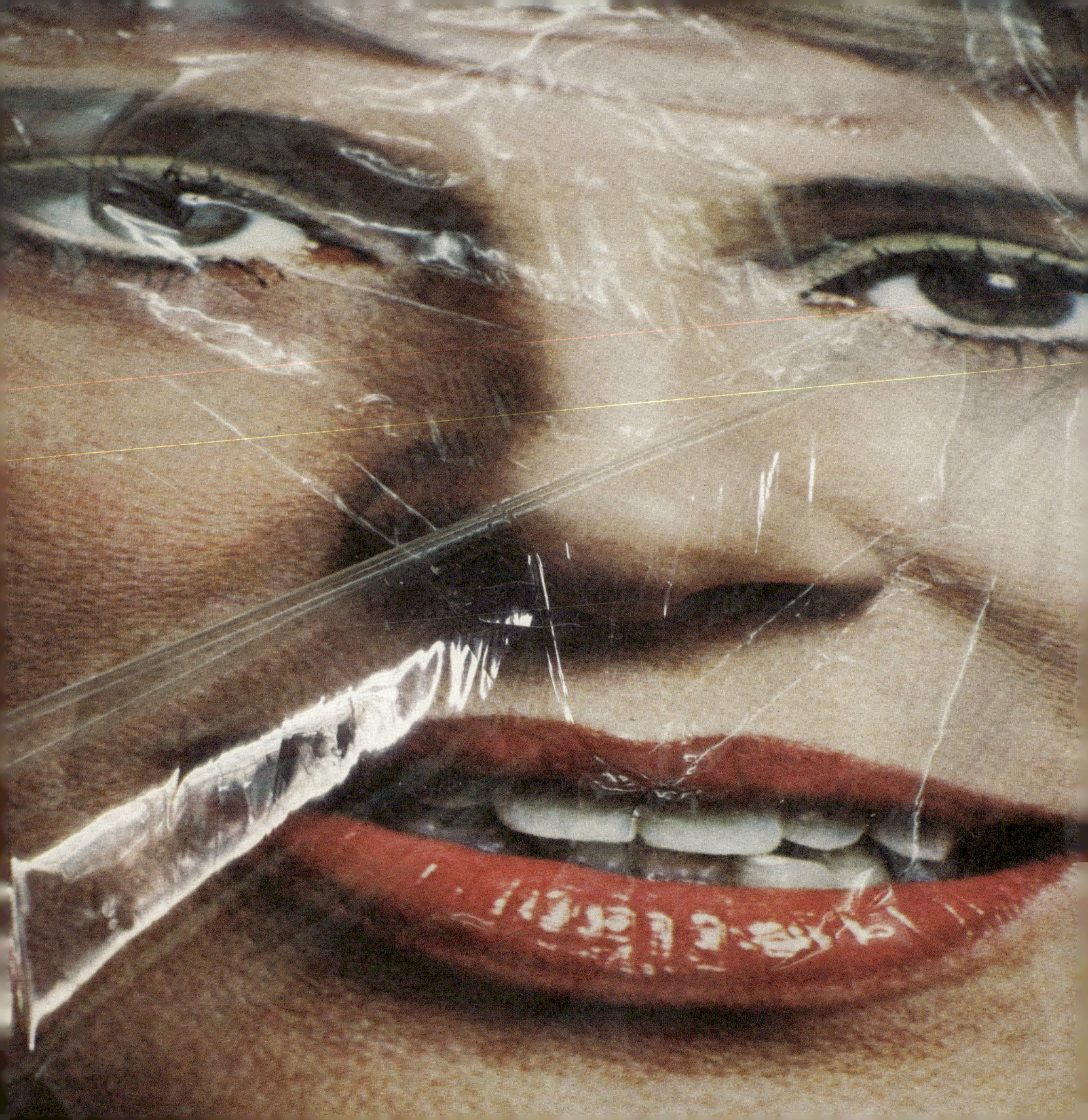

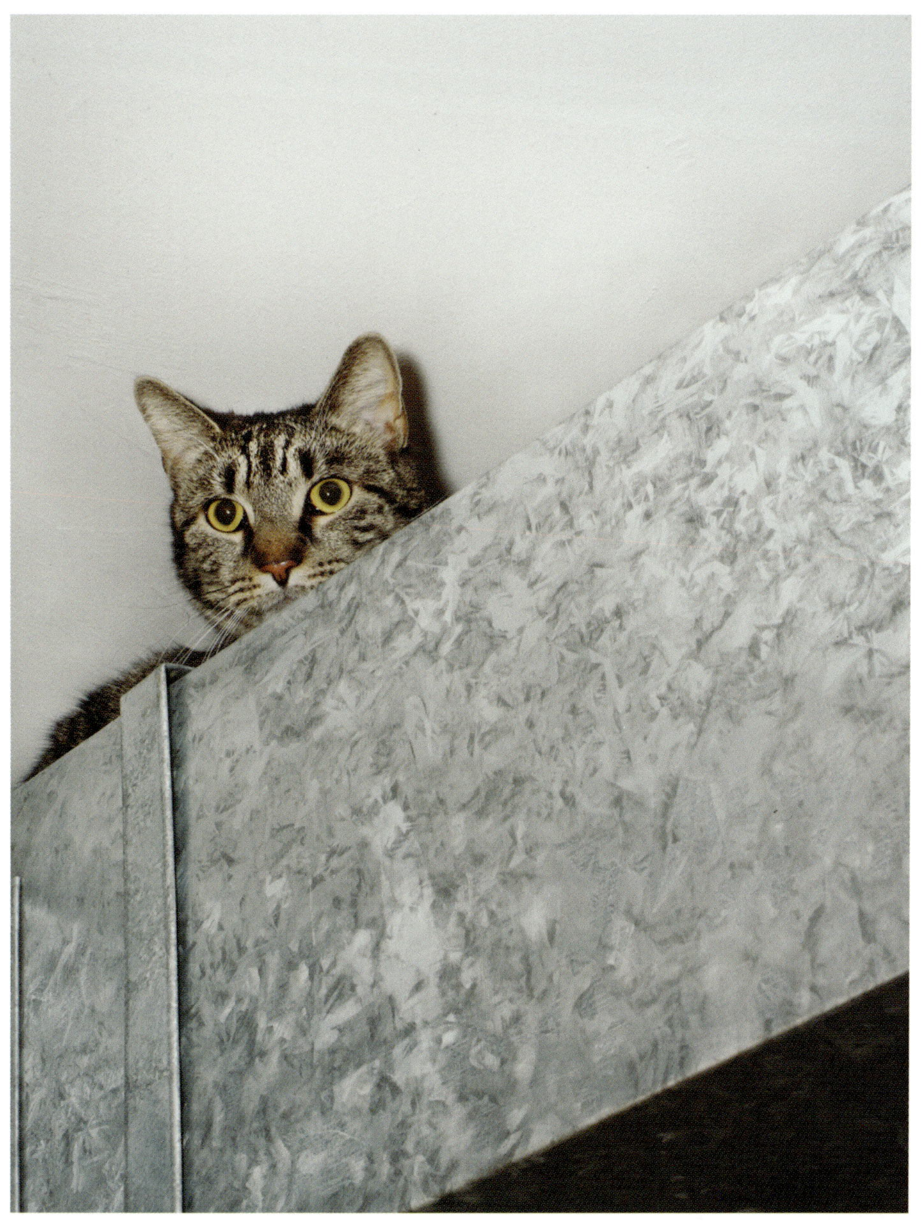

DEATH TAKES A HOLIDAY

BY DARIN MICKEY

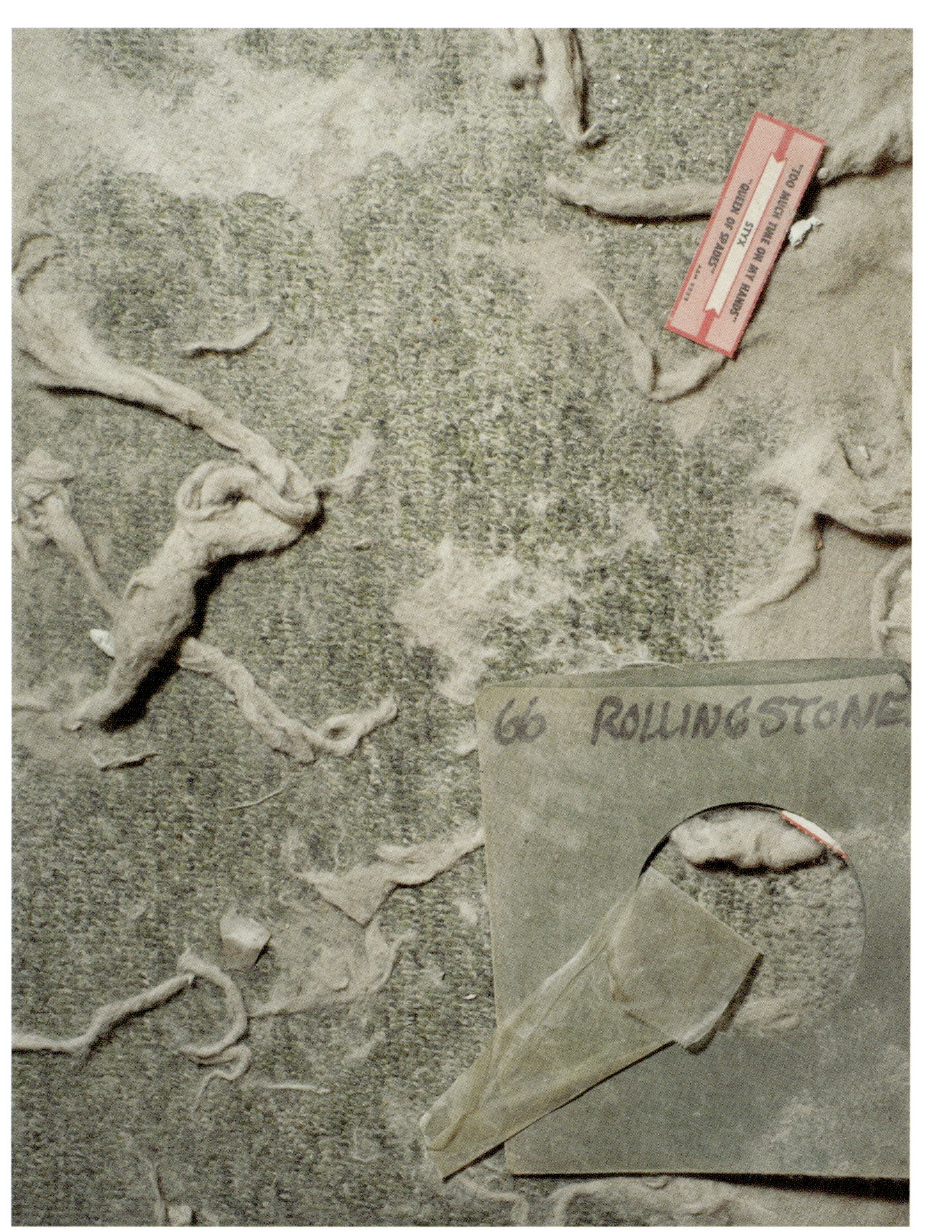

"TOO MUCH TIME ON MY HANDS"
STYX
"QUEEN OF SPADES"
66 ROLLINGSTONE

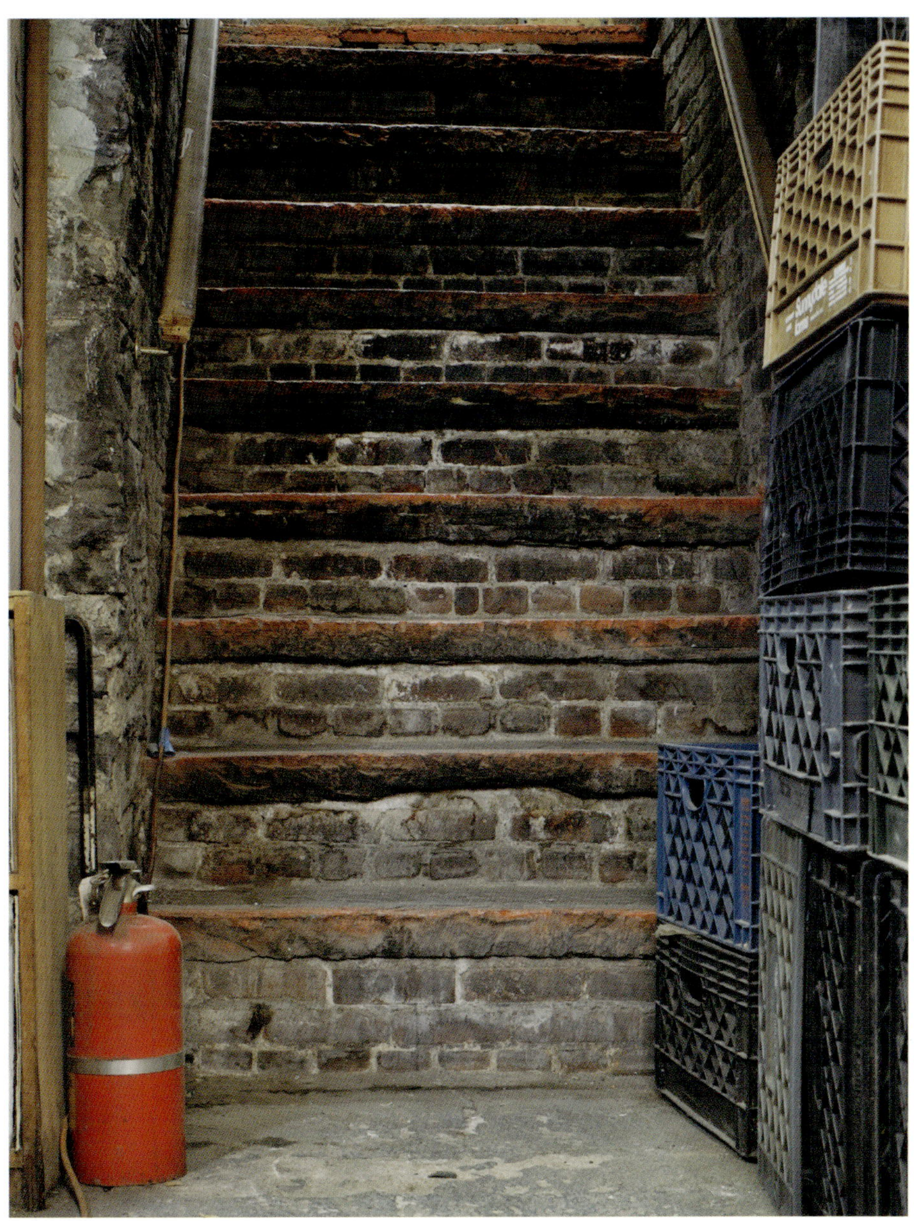

YOU KNOW, DESPITE WHAT YOU MIGHT'A
HEARD, I LIKE PEOPLE.

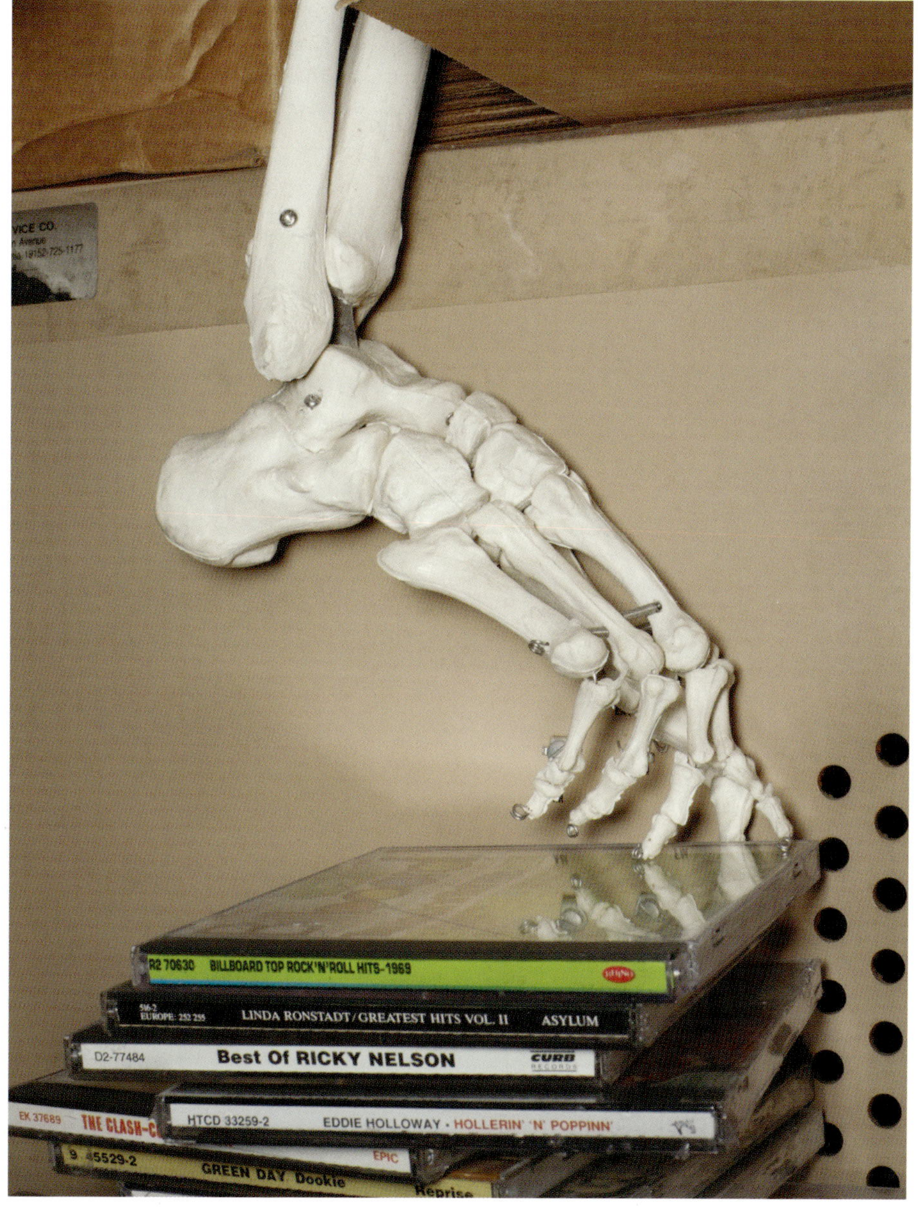
VICE CO.
n Avenue
a, 19152-725-1177
R2 70630   BILLBOARD TOP ROCK'N'ROLL HITS-1969   Rhino
516-2
EUROPE: 252 255   LINDA RONSTADT/GREATEST HITS VOL. II   ASYLUM
D2-77484   Best Of RICKY NELSON   CURB RECORDS
EK 37689   THE CLASH-C   HTCD 33259-2   EDDIE HOLLOWAY · HOLLERIN' 'N' POPPINN'
9 45529-2   GREEN DAY Dookie   EPIC   Reprise

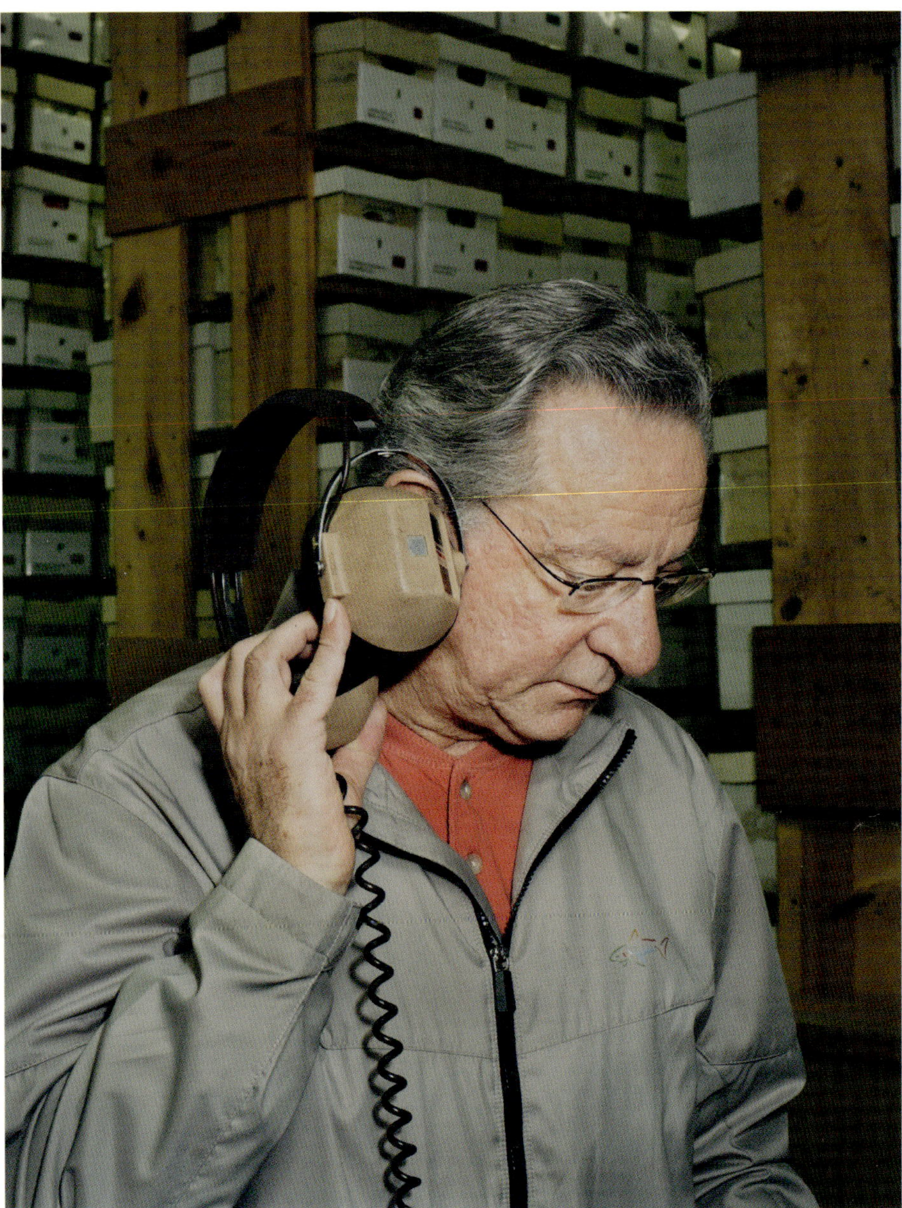

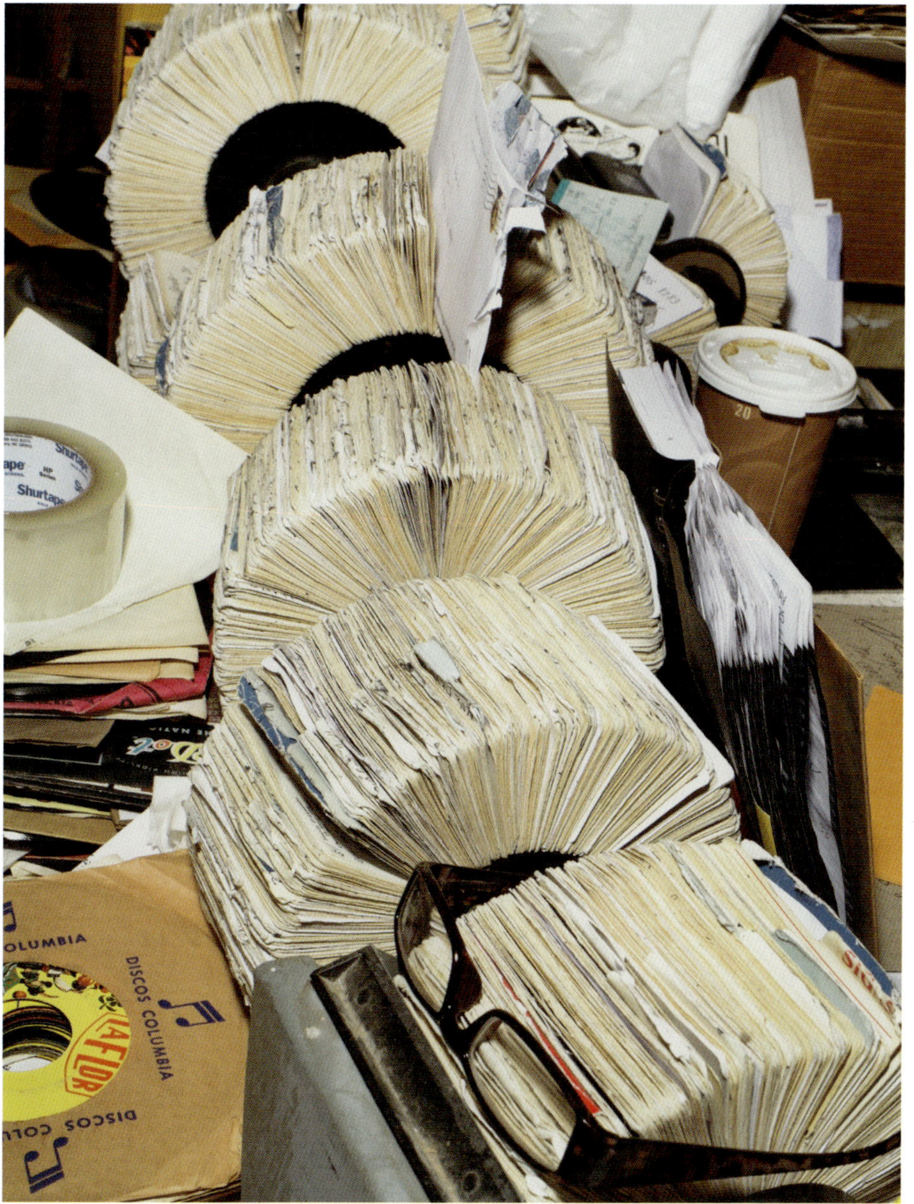

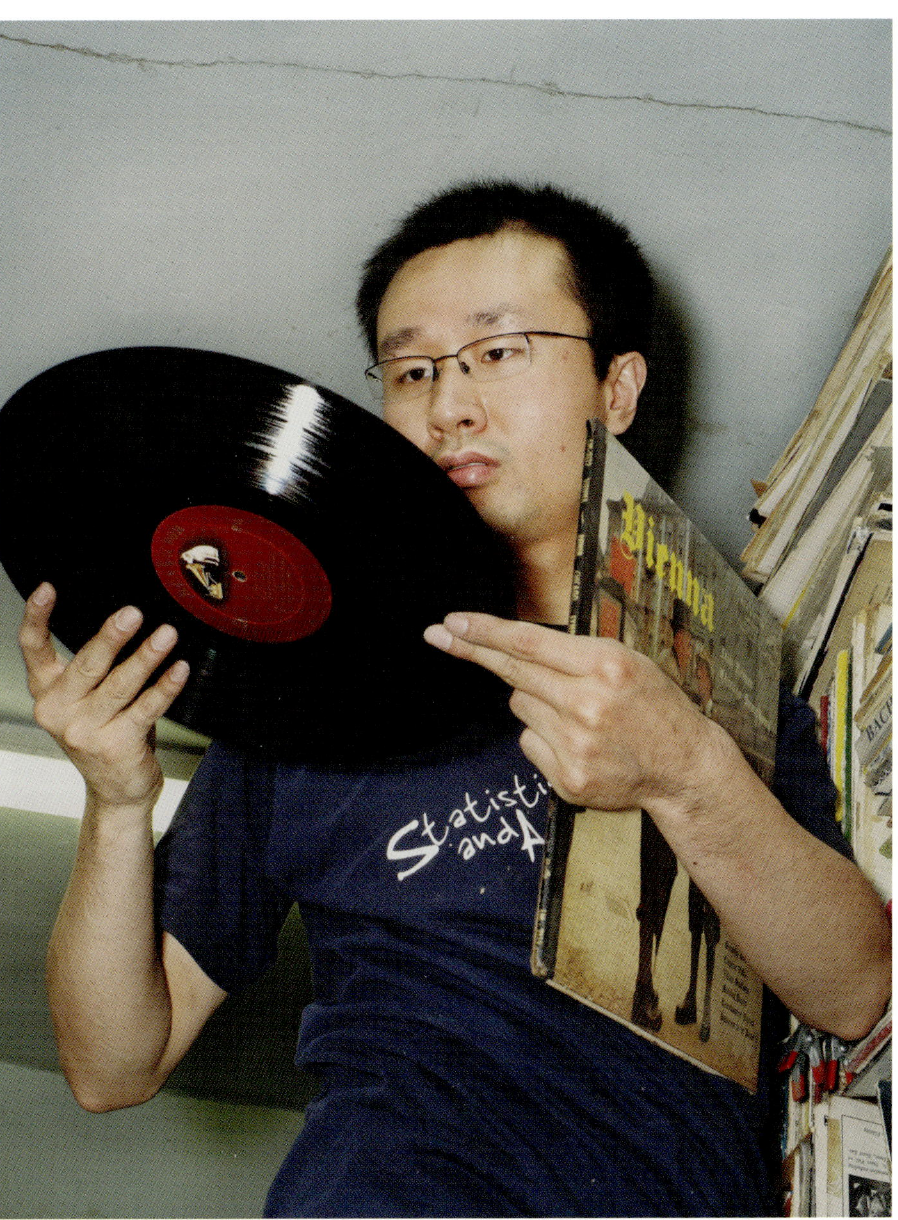

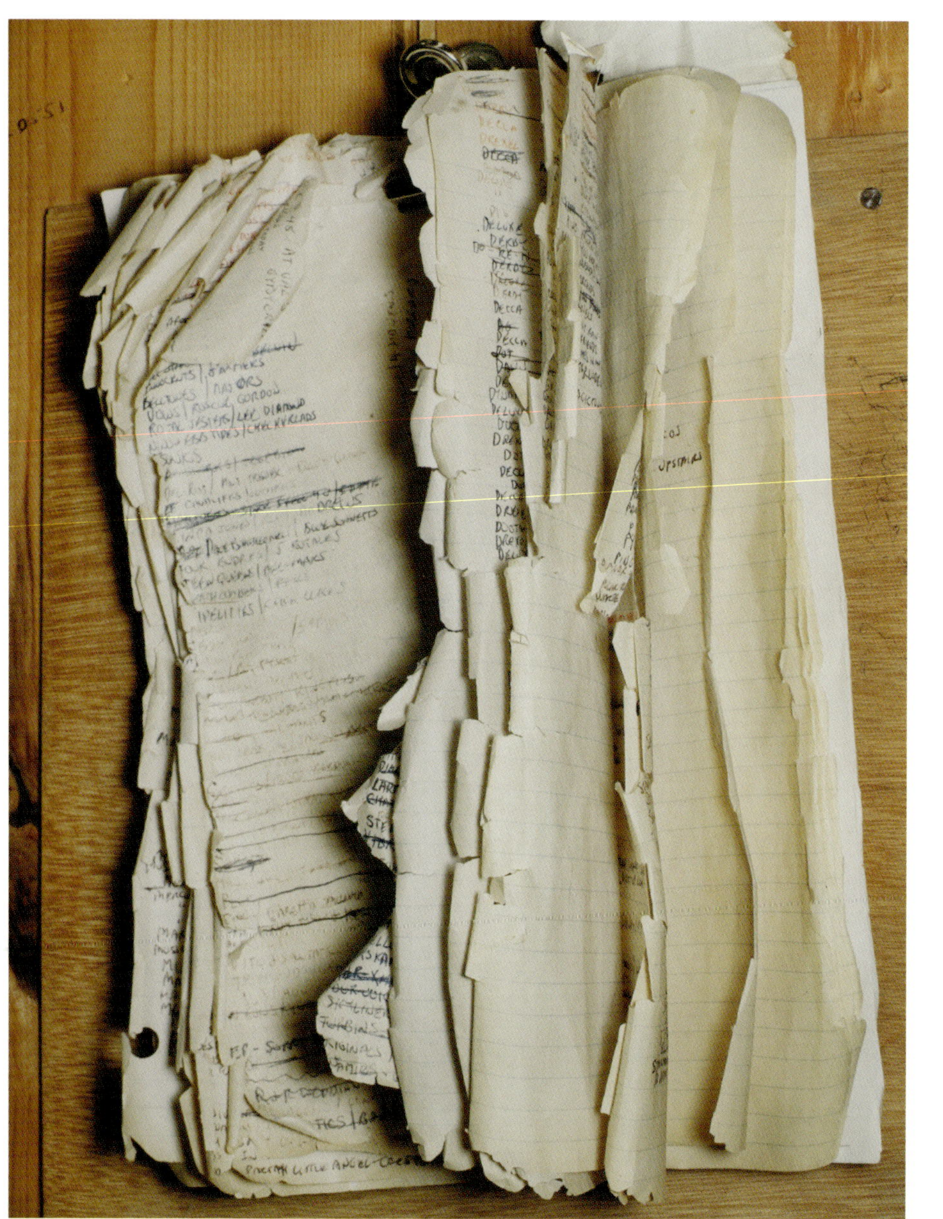

I WAS THE BUYER.
I WAS THE HIRER AND FIRER.

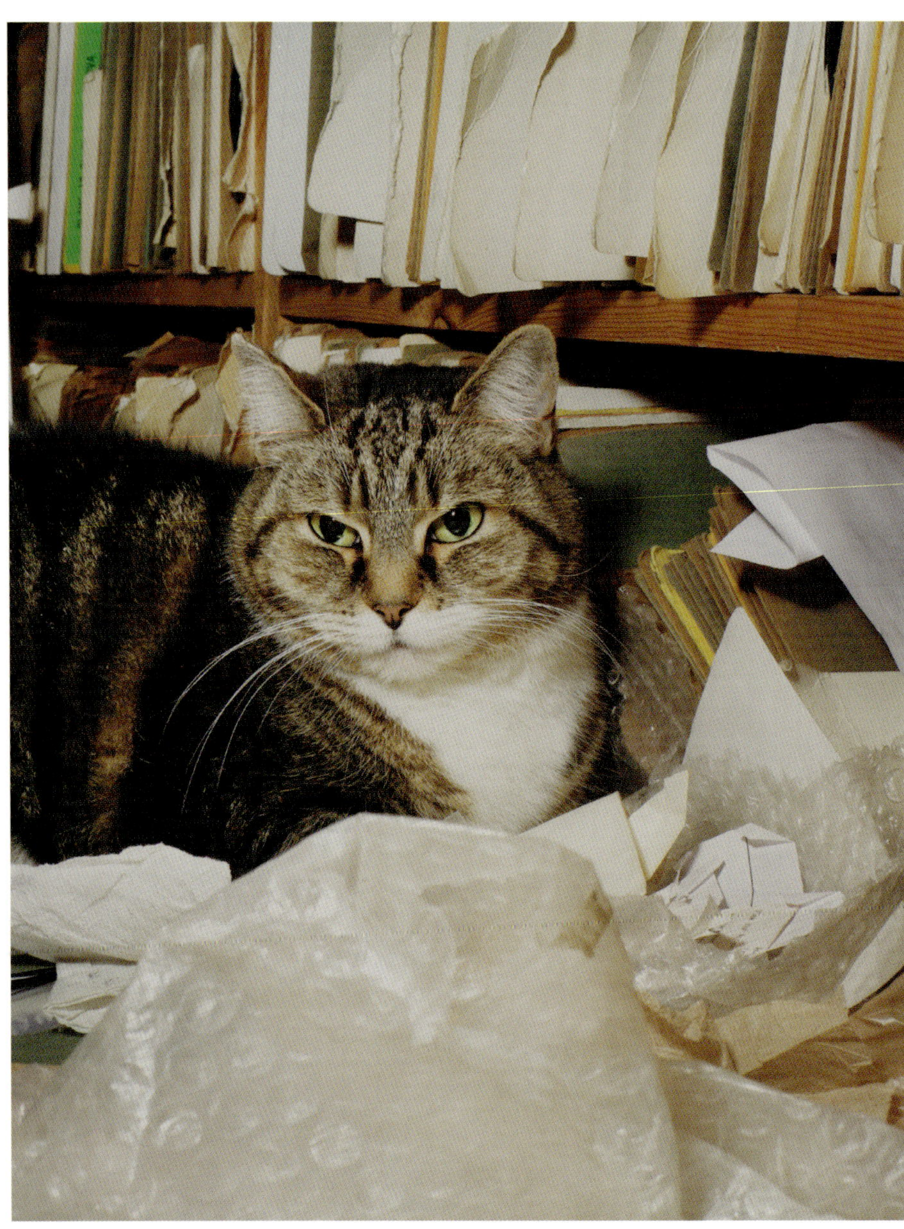

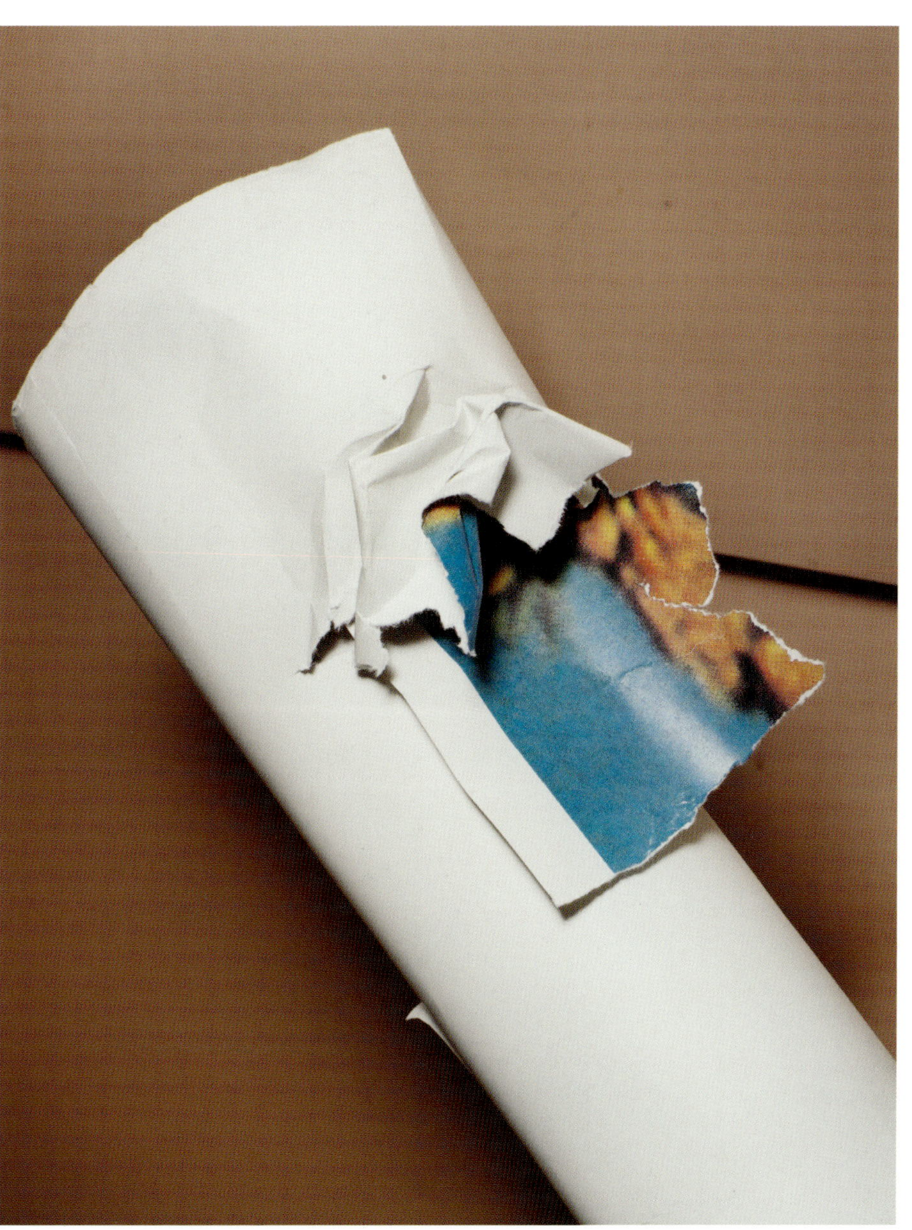

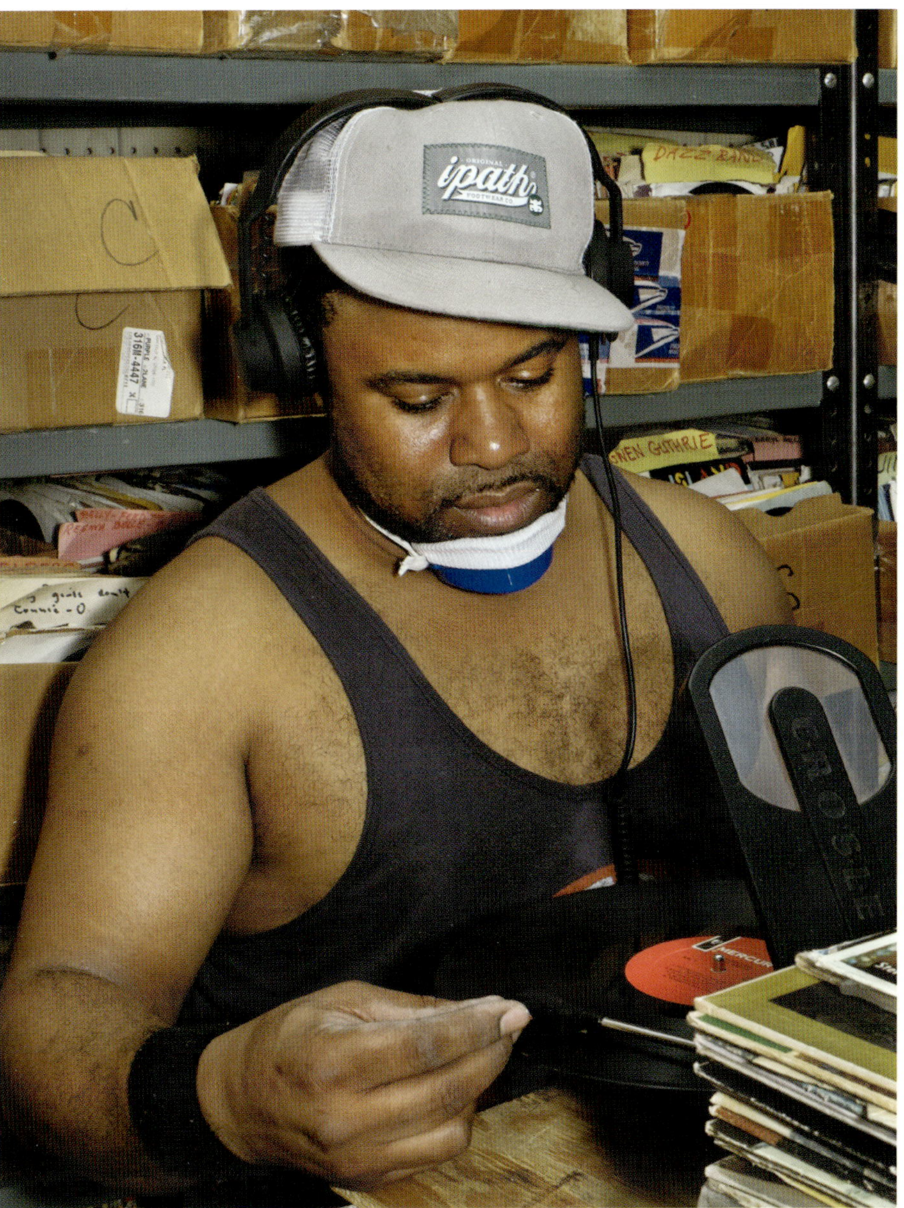

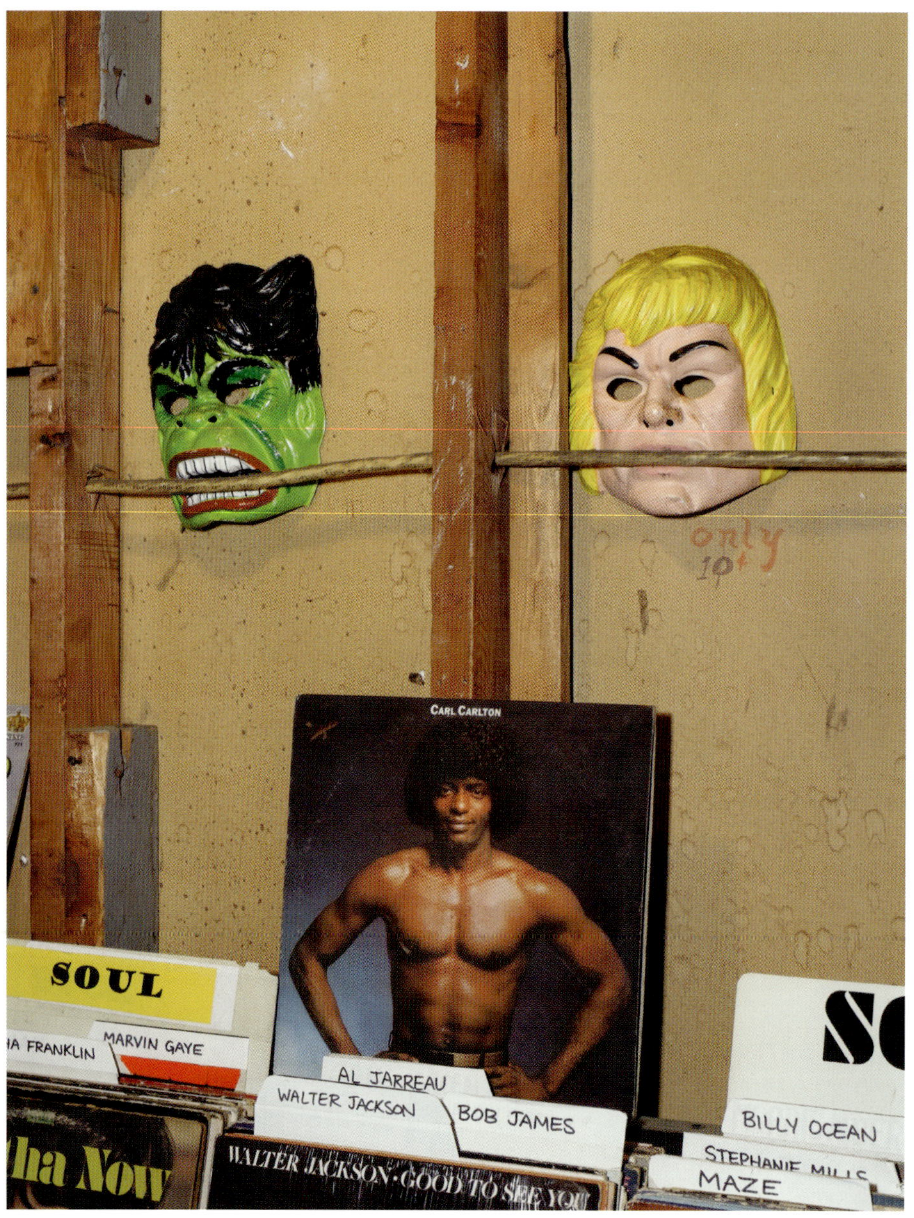

only
10¢
CARL CARLTON
SOUL
SO
ha FRANKLIN
MARVIN GAYE
AL JARREAU
WALTER JACKSON
BOB JAMES
BILLY OCEAN
STEPHANIE MILLS
MAZE
ha Now
WALTER JACKSON · GOOD TO SEE YOU

HE REMINDS ME, DEFINITELY, OF ME.

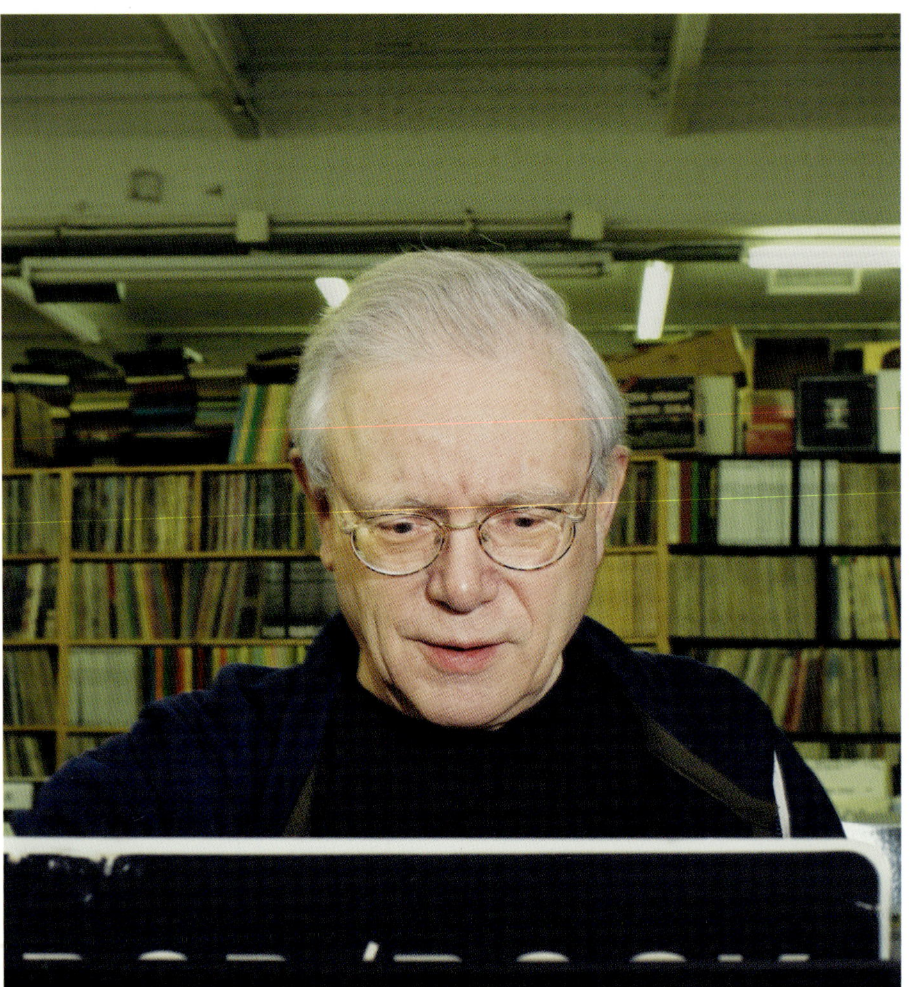
GOSPEL

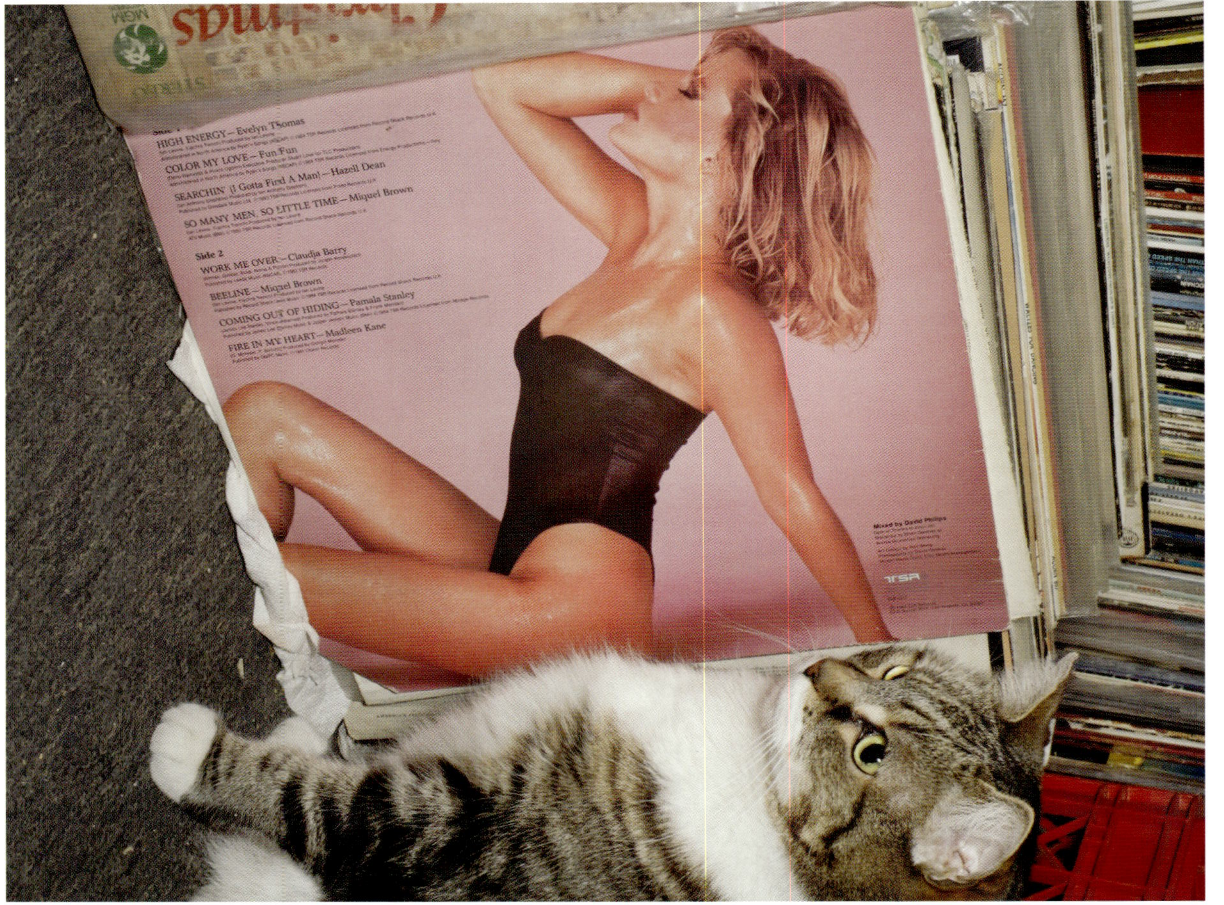
Side 1
HIGH ENERGY — Evelyn Thomas
COLOR MY LOVE — Fun Fun
SEARCHIN' (I Gotta Find A Man) — Hazell Dean
SO MANY MEN, SO LITTLE TIME — Miquel Brown
Side 2
WORK ME OVER — Claudja Barry
BEELINE — Miquel Brown
COMING OUT OF HIDING — Pamala Stanley
FIRE IN MY HEART — Madleen Kane
Mixed by David Phillips
TSR

I SAYS, "HOW 'BOUT A QUARTER A PIECE?"

SHE GOES,

"HAVE FUN.

JUST MAKE SURE YOU DON'T
FALL THROUGH THE FLOOR.

YOU GOTTA GO WHERE
THERE'S BEAMS."

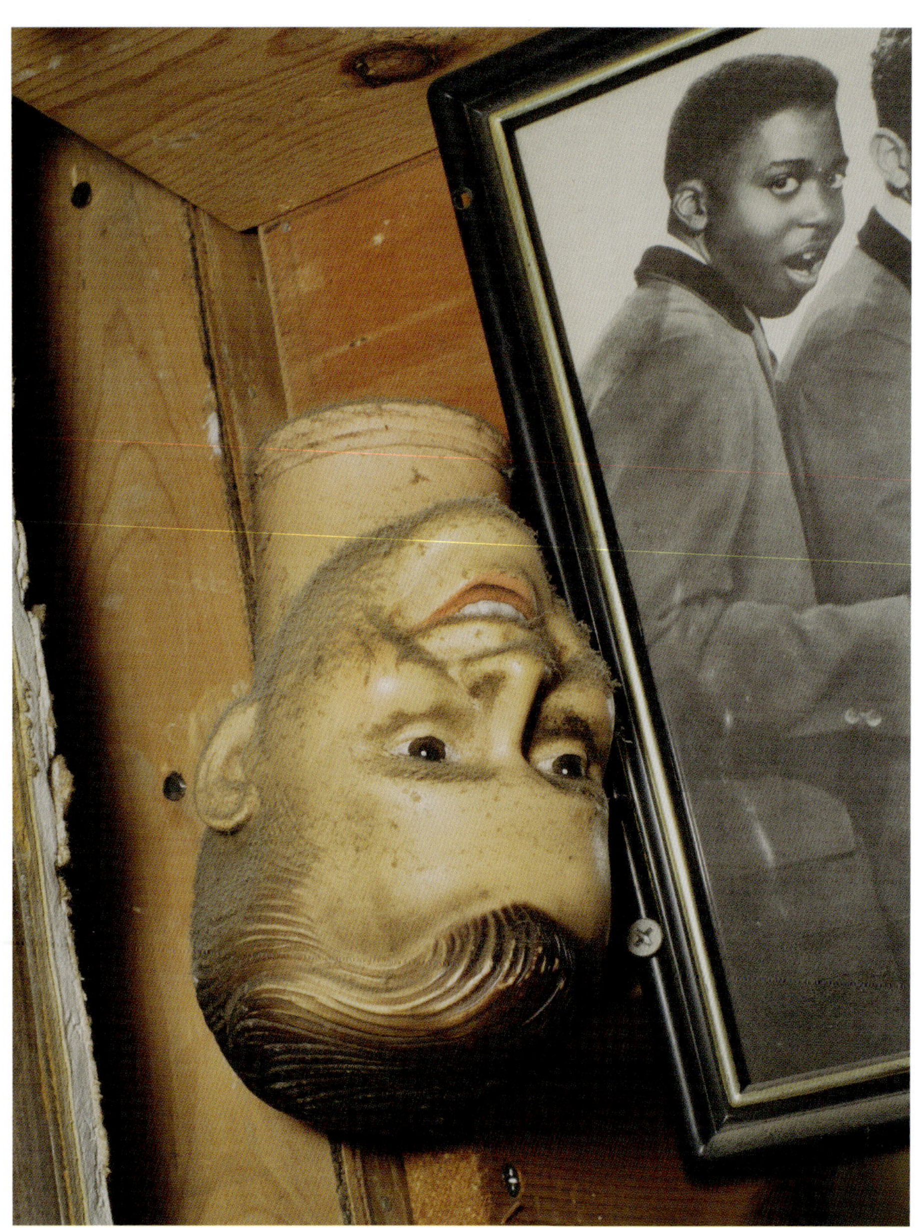

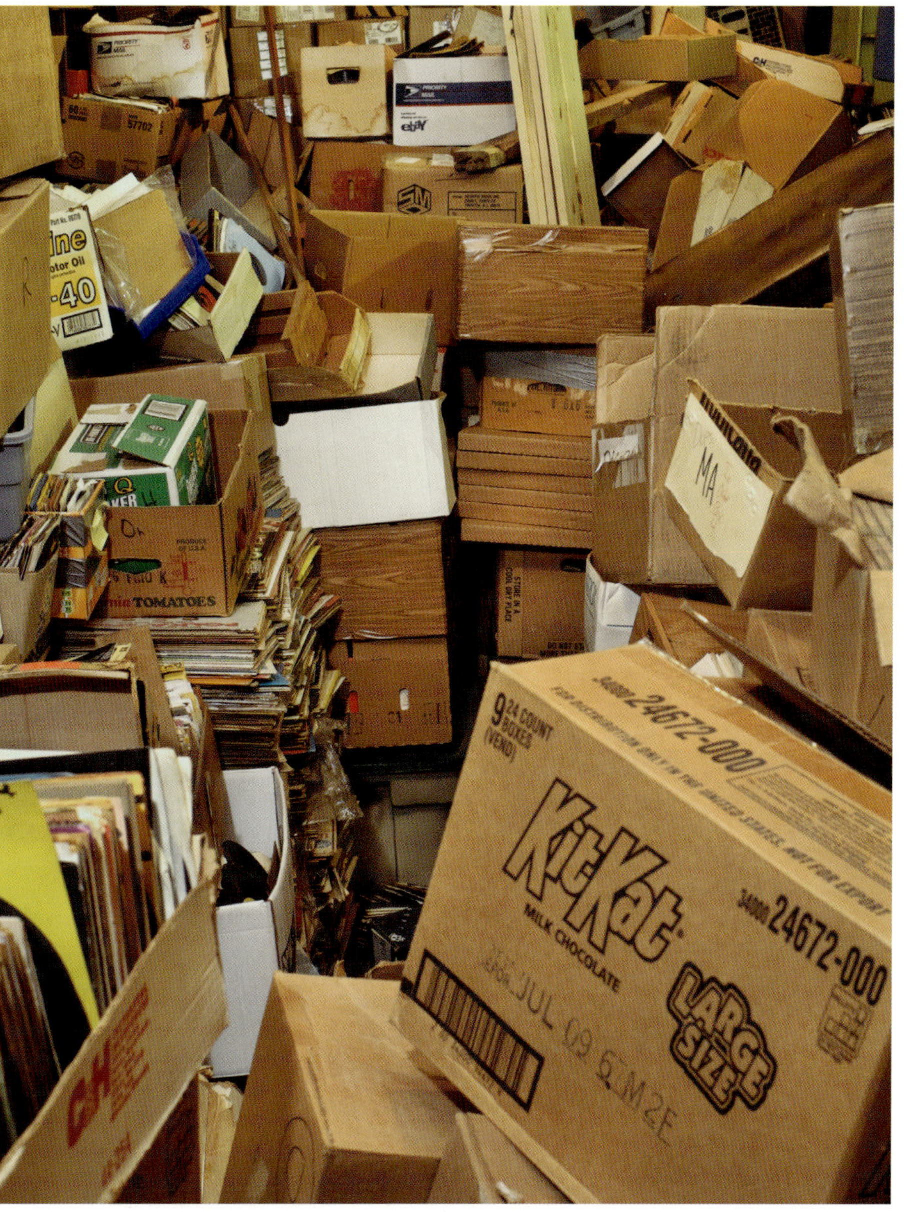

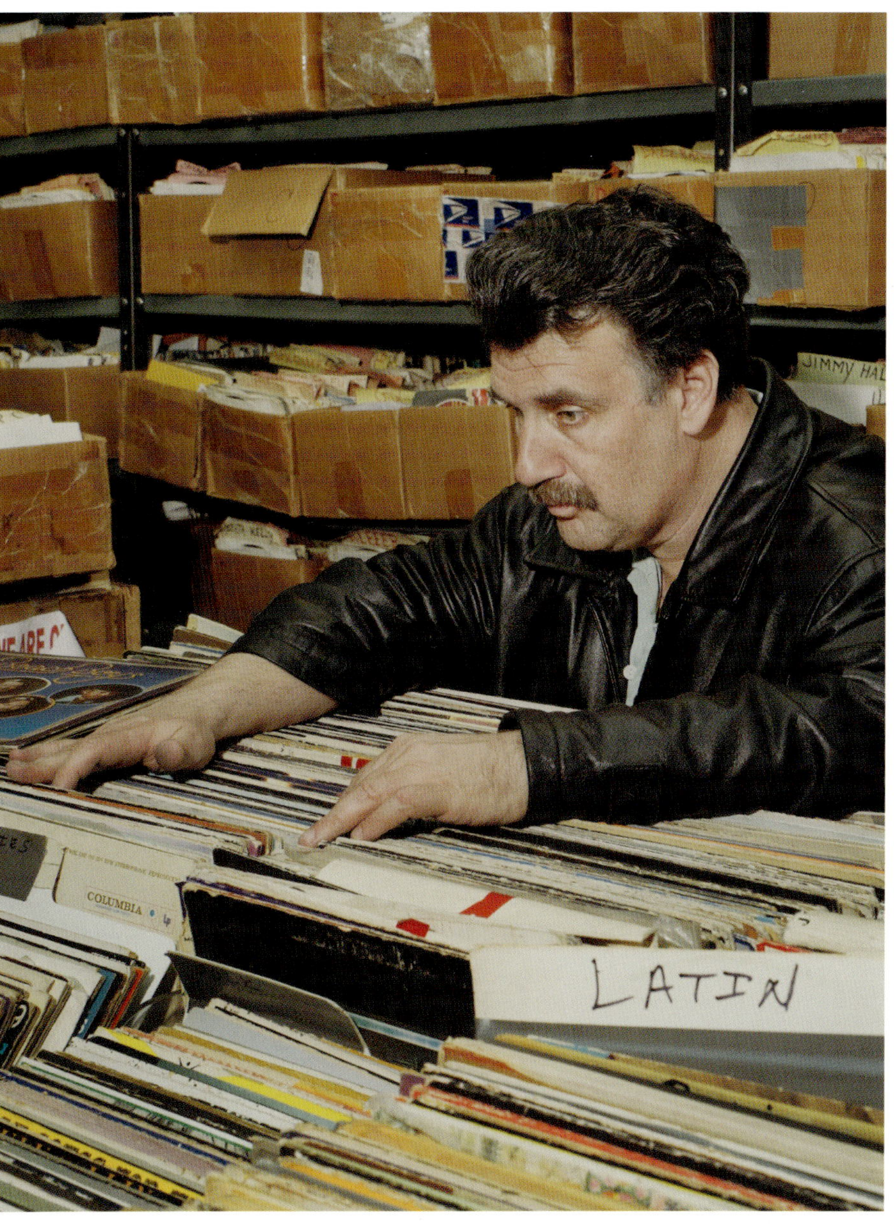

JIMMY HAL
COLUMBIA
LATIN

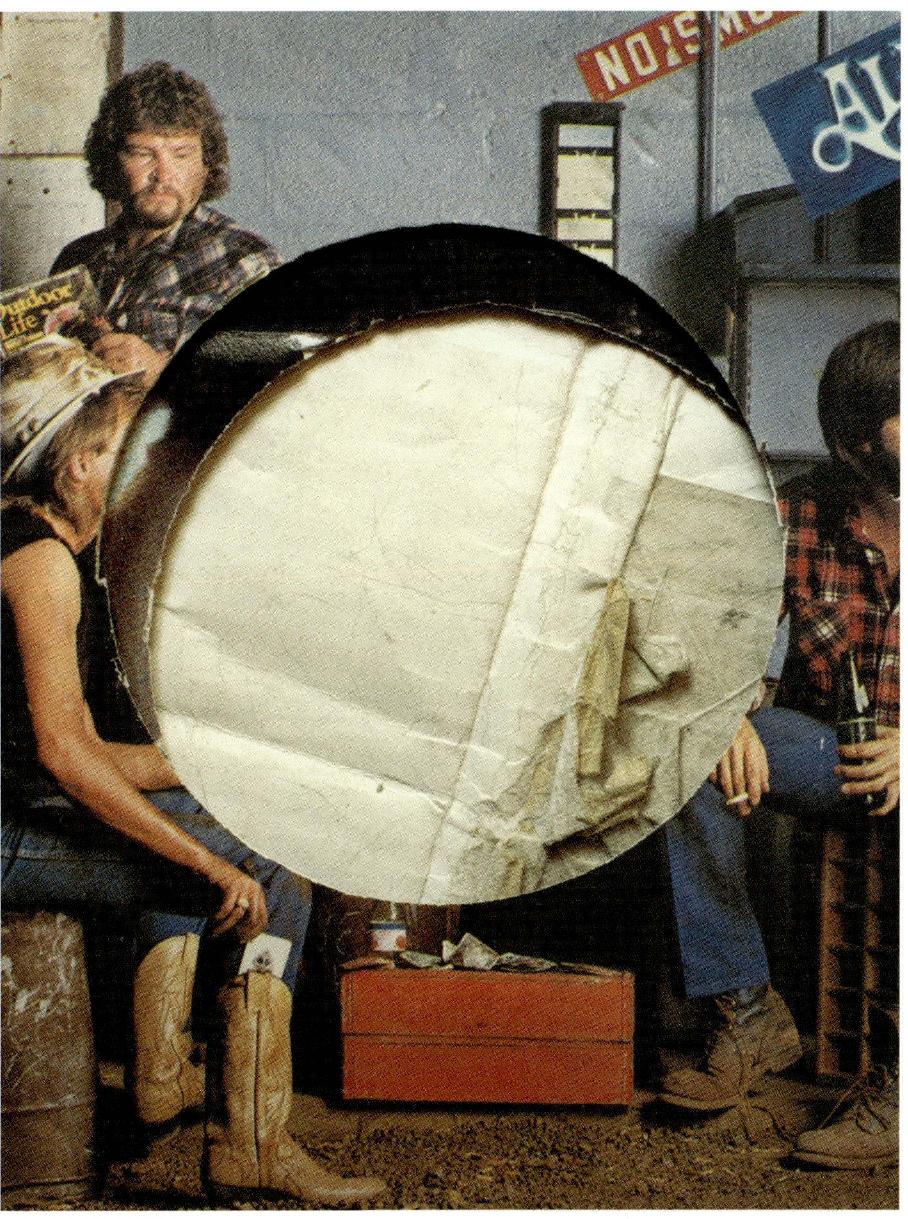

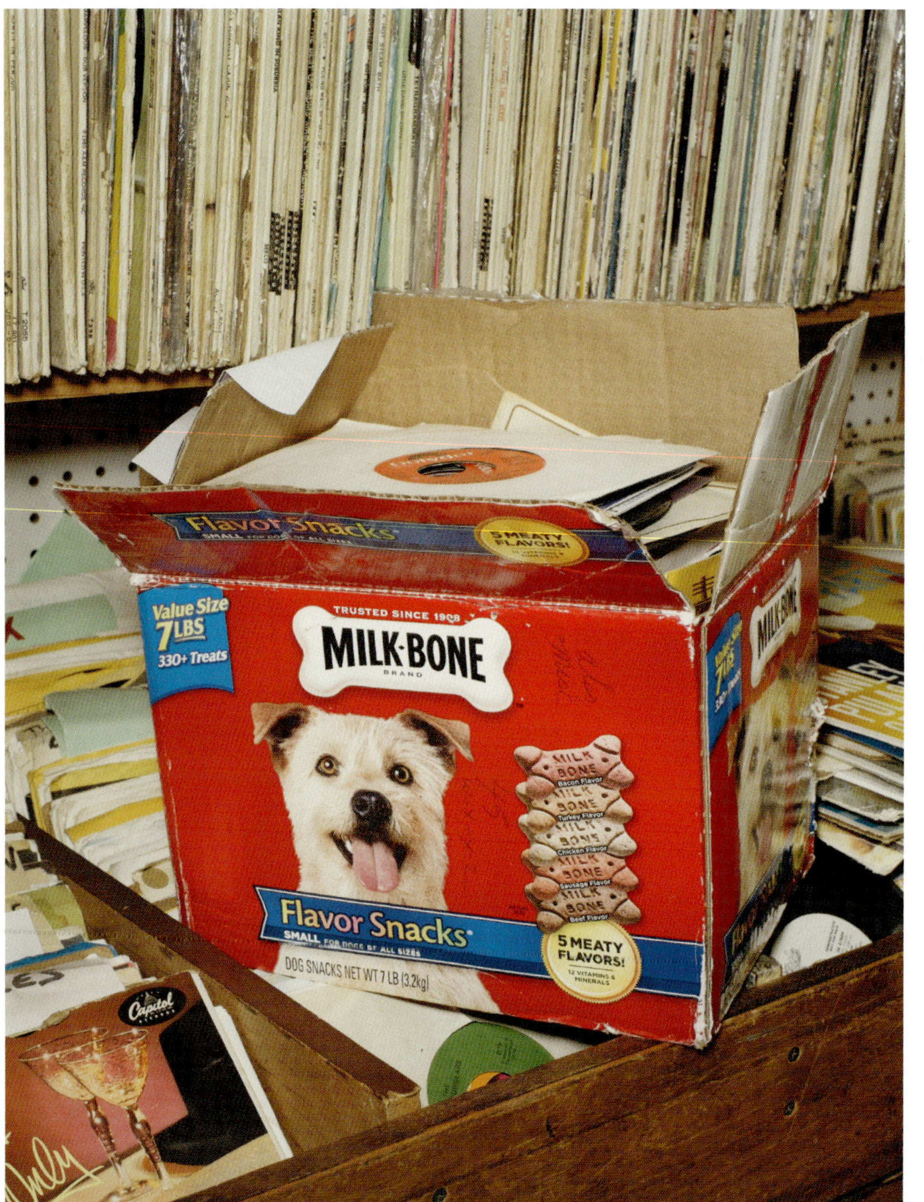

Flavor Snacks
SMALL FOR DOGS OF ALL SIZES
5 MEATY FLAVORS!
Value Size 7 LBS
330+ Treats
TRUSTED SINCE 1908
MILK·BONE
BRAND
MILK BONE Bacon Flavor
MILK BONE Turkey Flavor
MILK BONE Chicken Flavor
MILK BONE Sausage Flavor
MILK BONE Beef Flavor
Flavor Snacks
SMALL FOR DOGS OF ALL SIZES
DOG SNACKS NET WT 7 LB (3.2kg)
5 MEATY FLAVORS!
12 VITAMINS & MINERALS
MILK·BONE
Capitol RECORDS

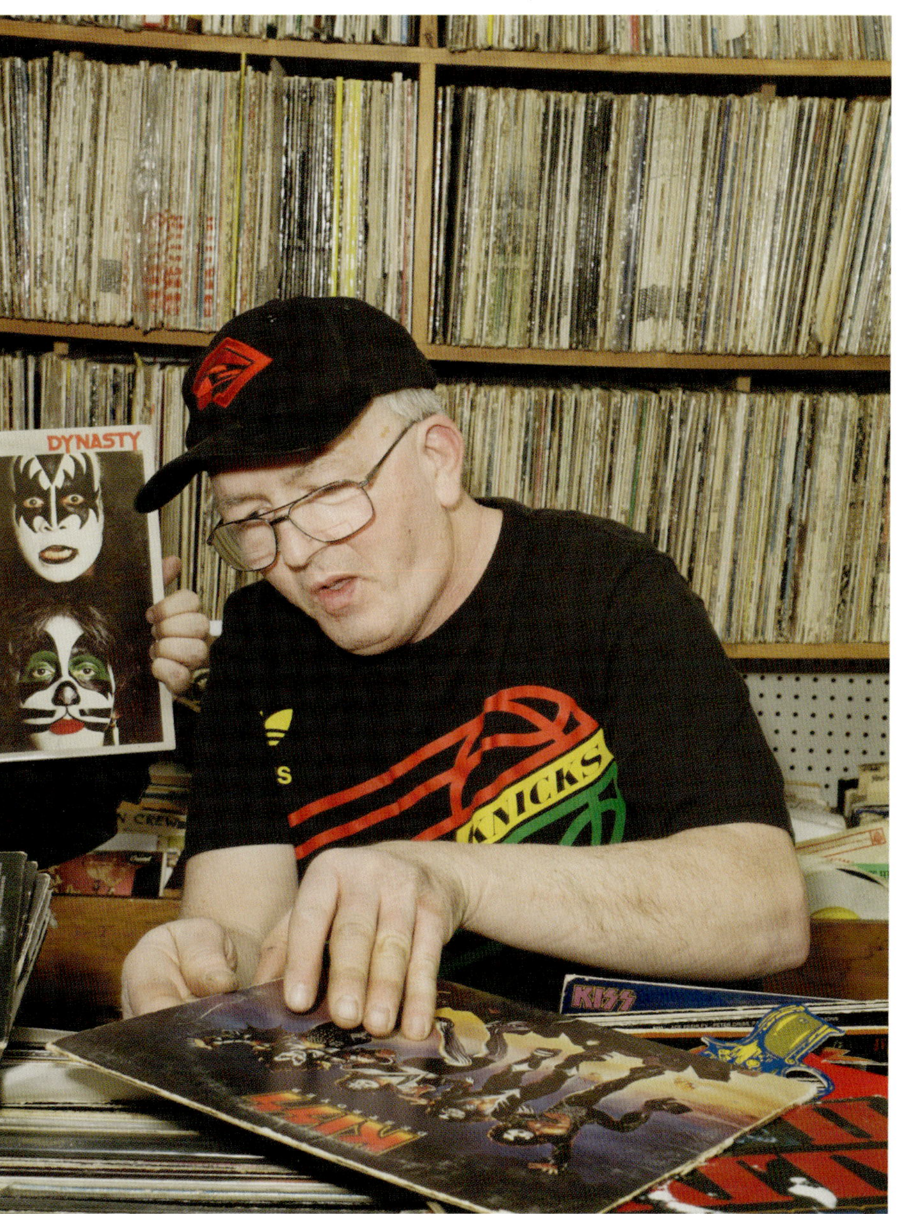

SHE'S TELLING ME, YOU KNOW,

"GET WITH ME HONEY AND YOU'LL
FORGET ALL ABOUT THESE RECORDS."

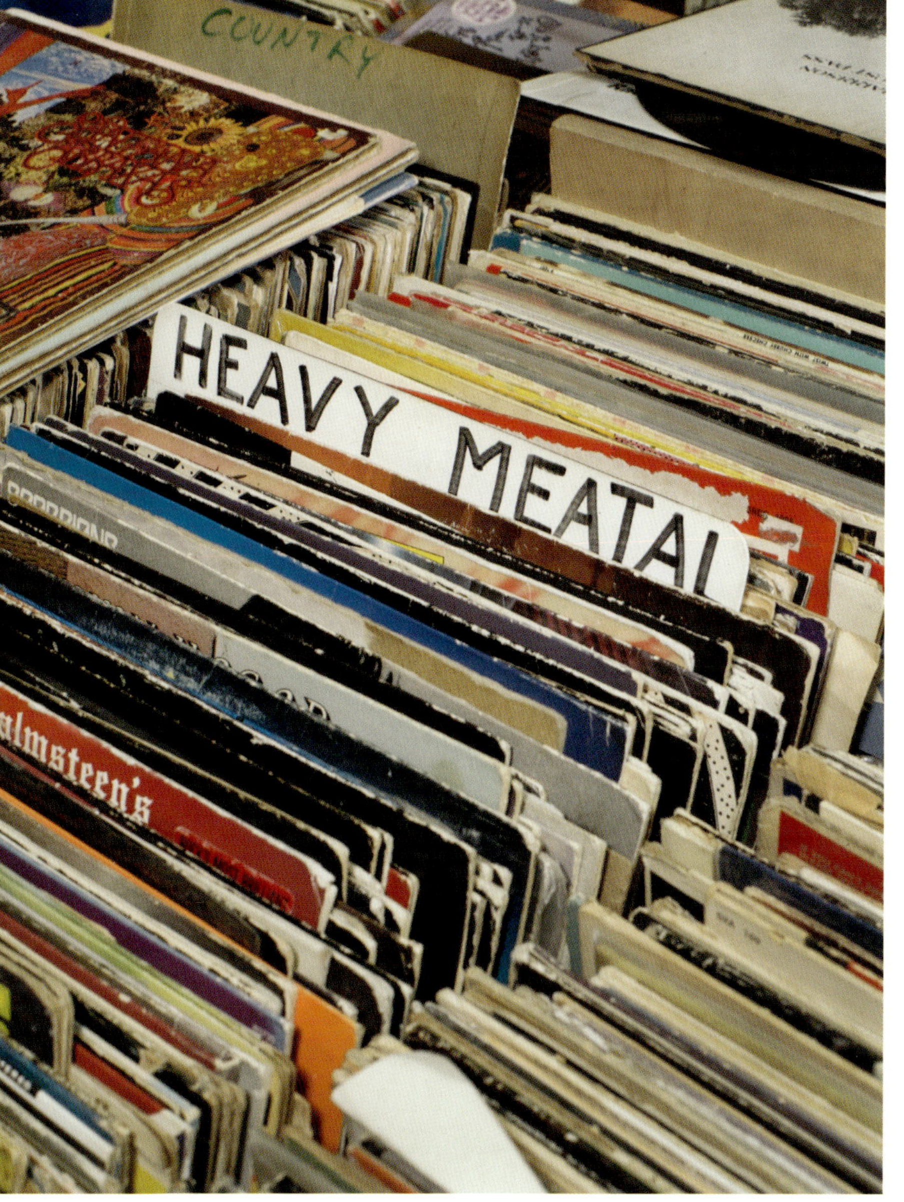

COUNTRY
HEAVY MEATAL
almsteen's

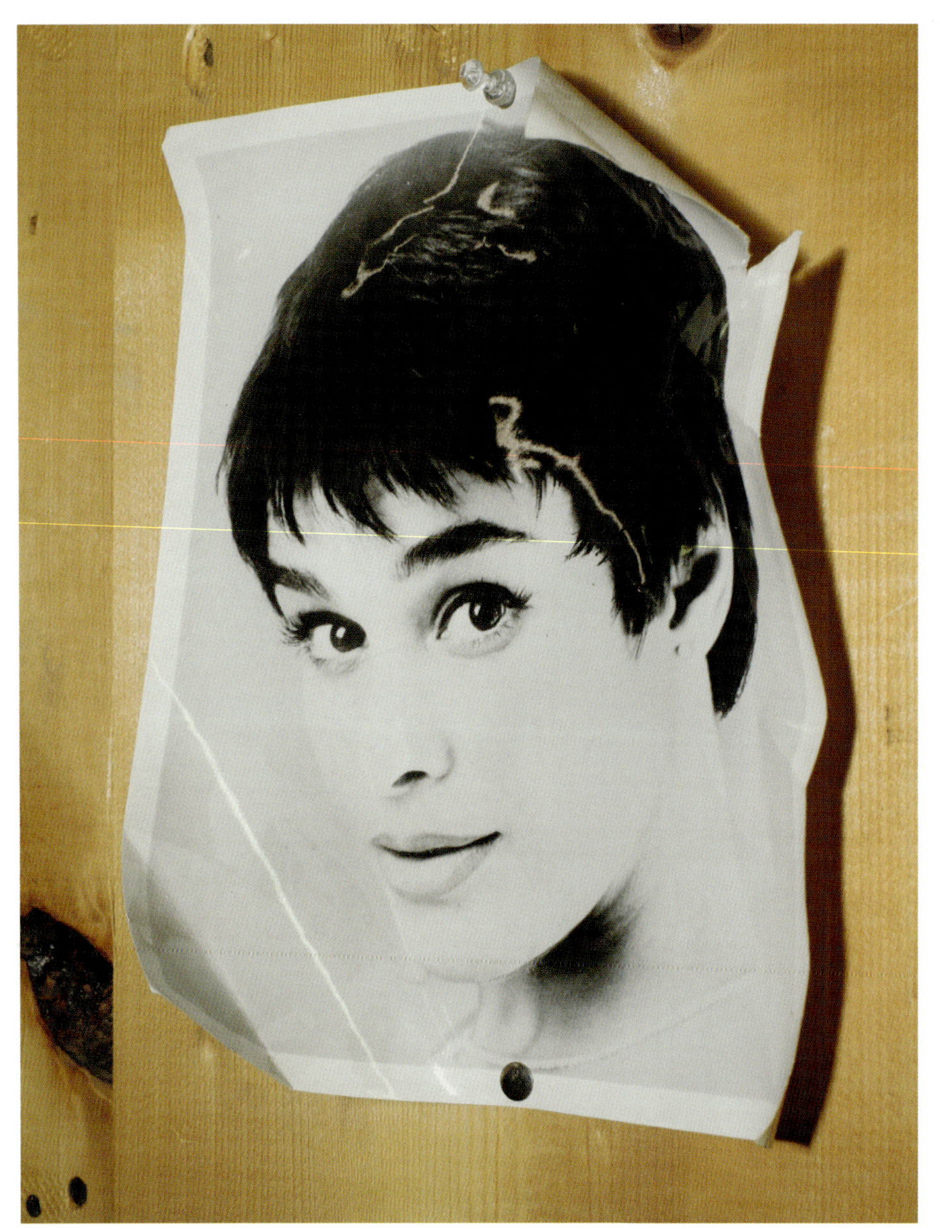

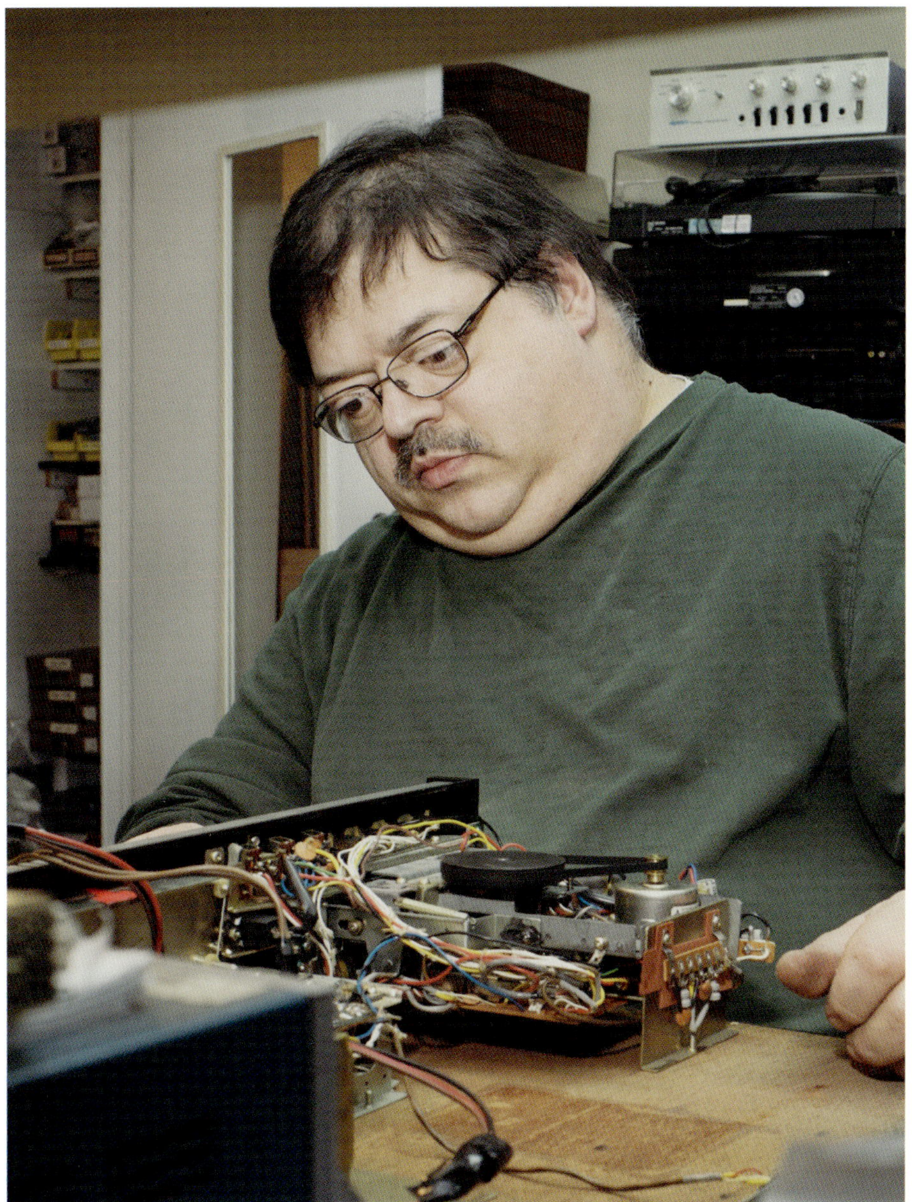

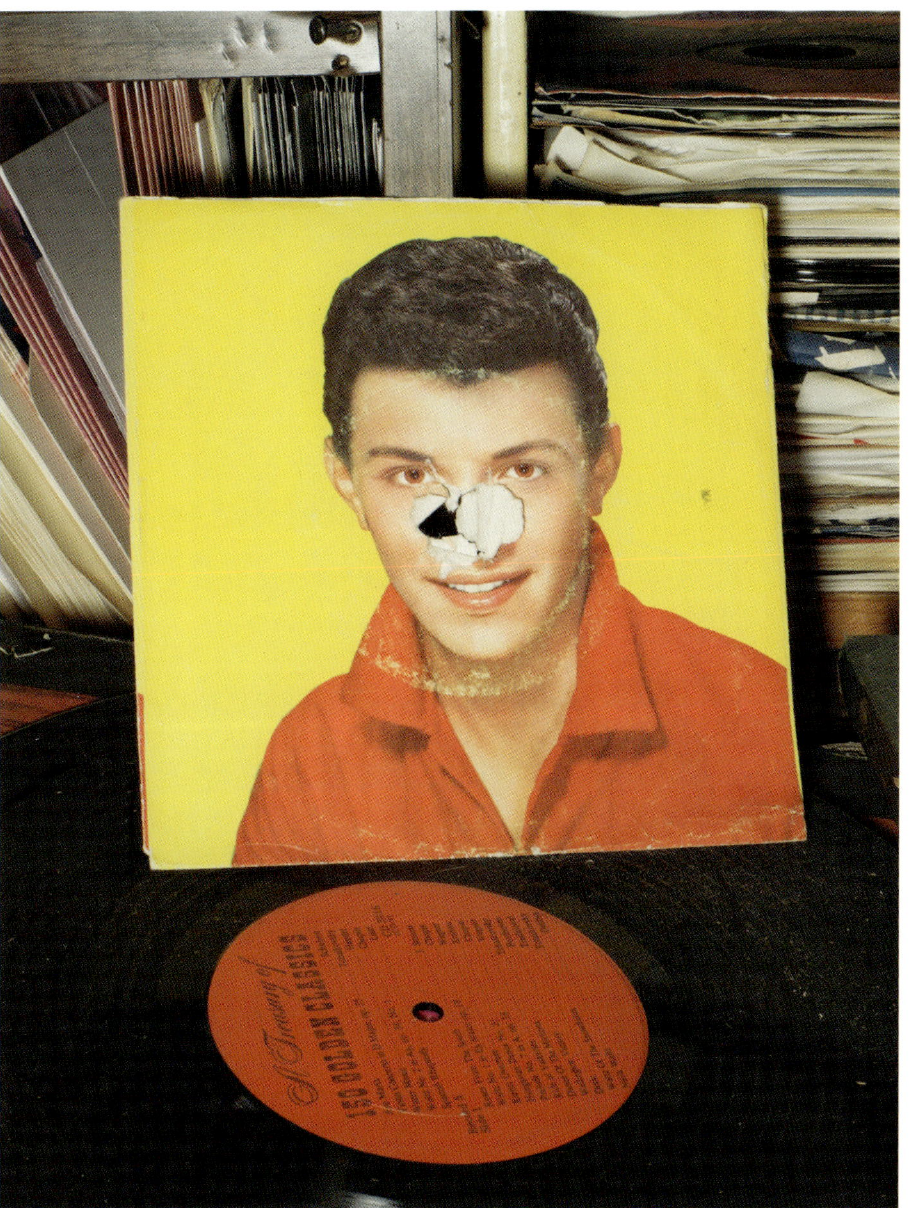

A Treasury of
50 GOLDEN CLASSICS

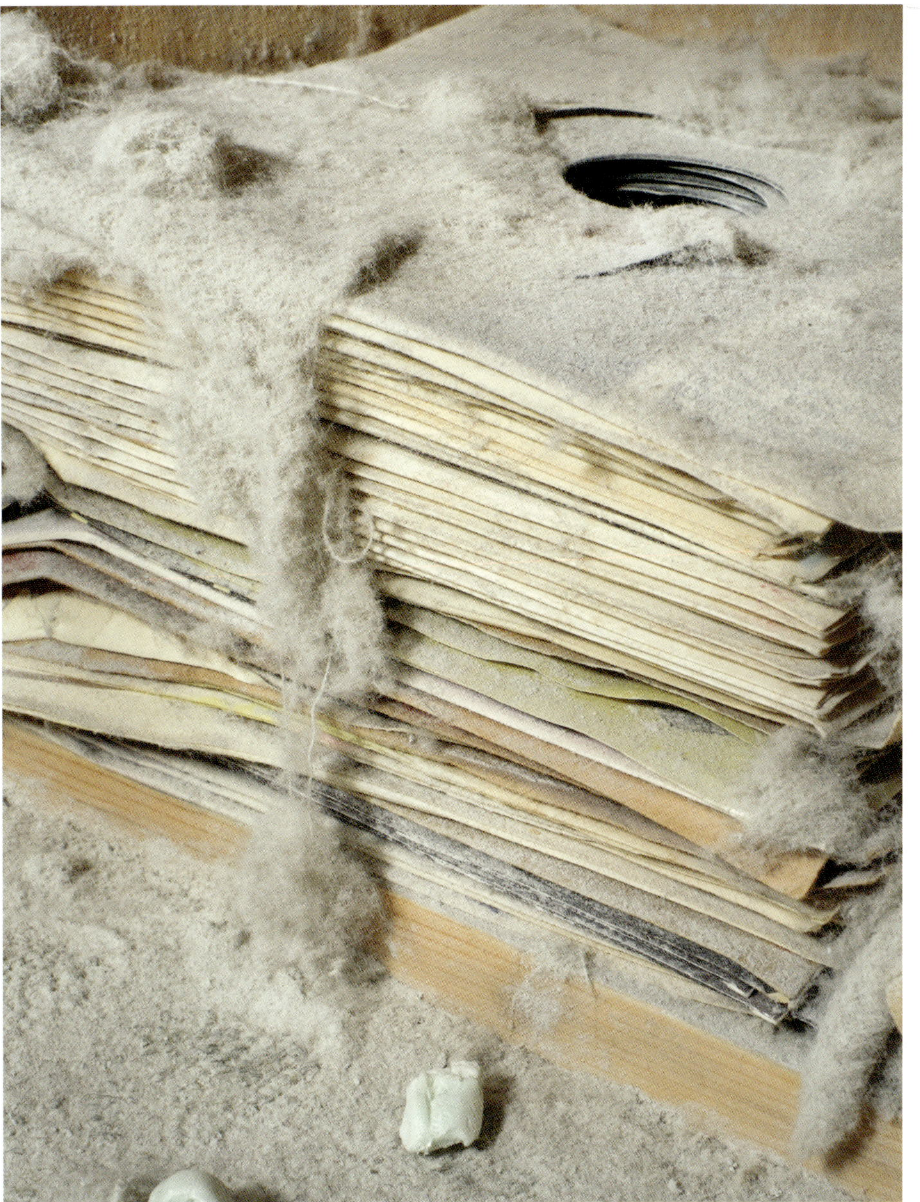

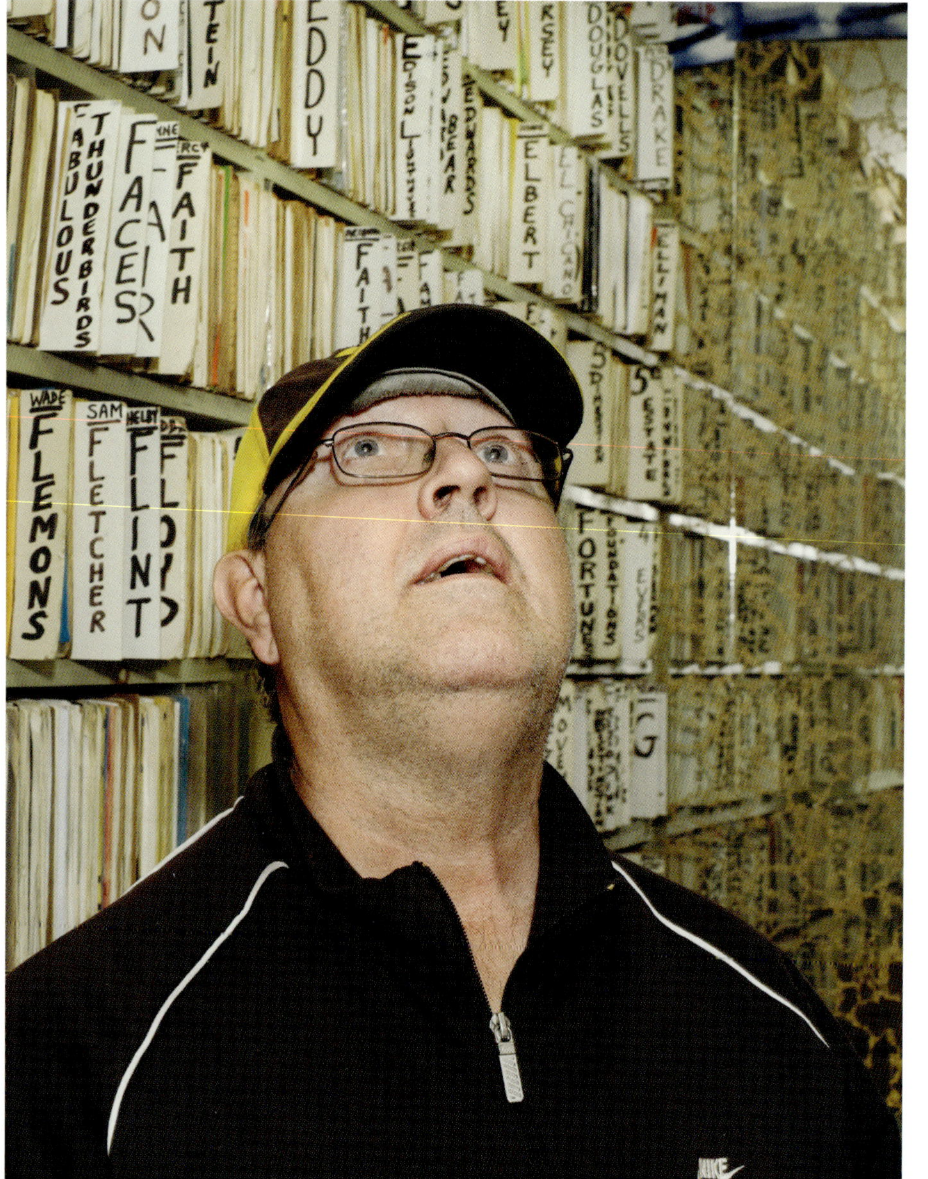

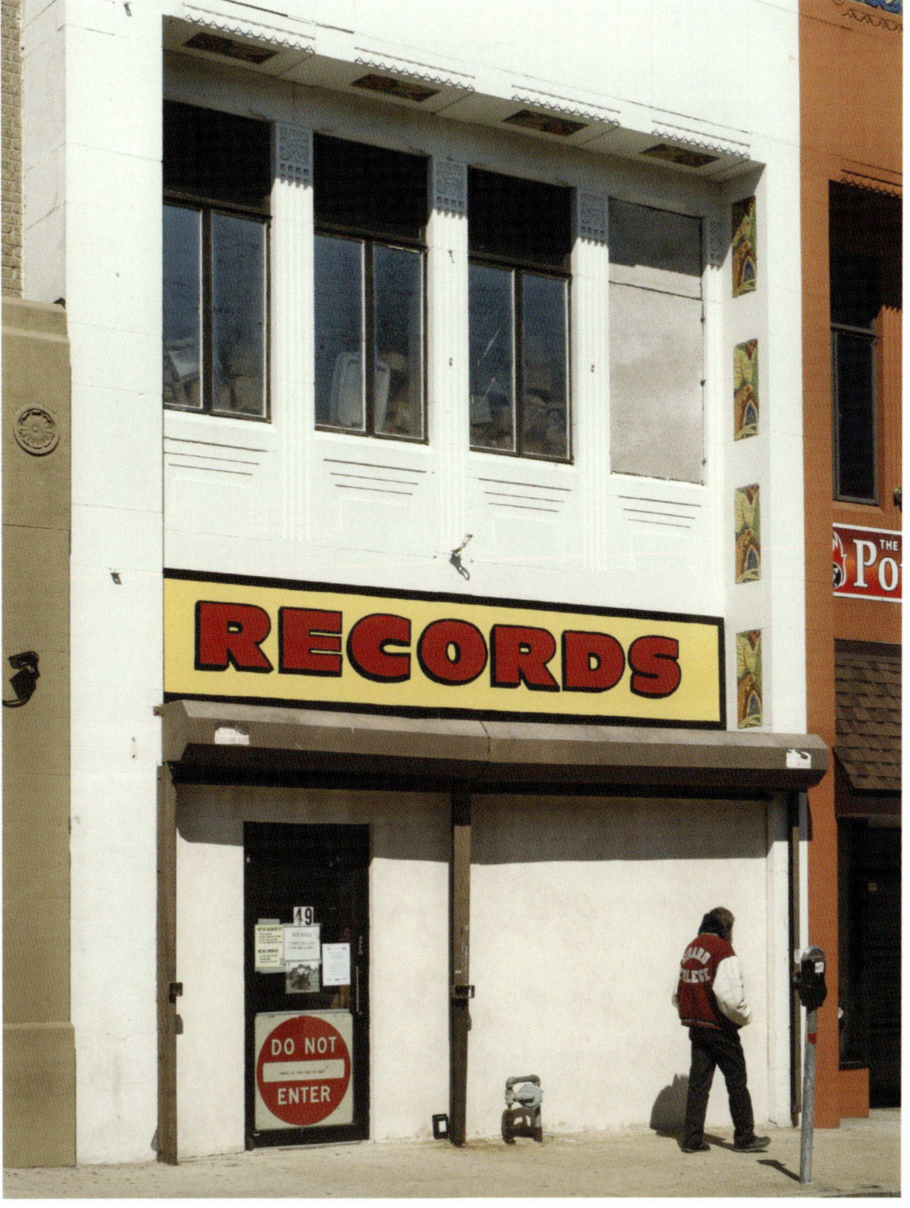
RECORDS
49
DO NOT
ENTER

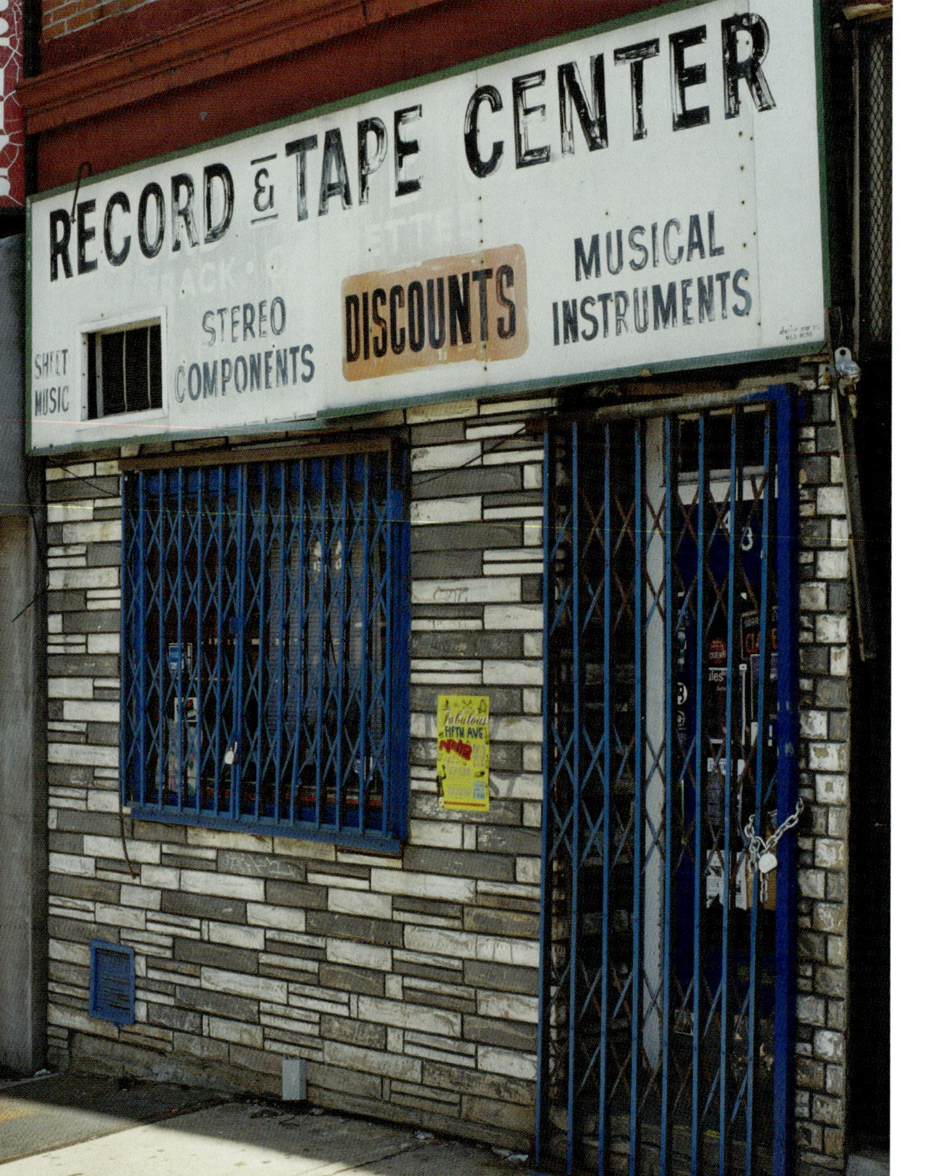
RECORD & TAPE CENTER
STEREO
COMPONENTS
DISCOUNTS
MUSICAL
INSTRUMENTS
SHEET
MUSIC
Fabulous
FIFTH AVE

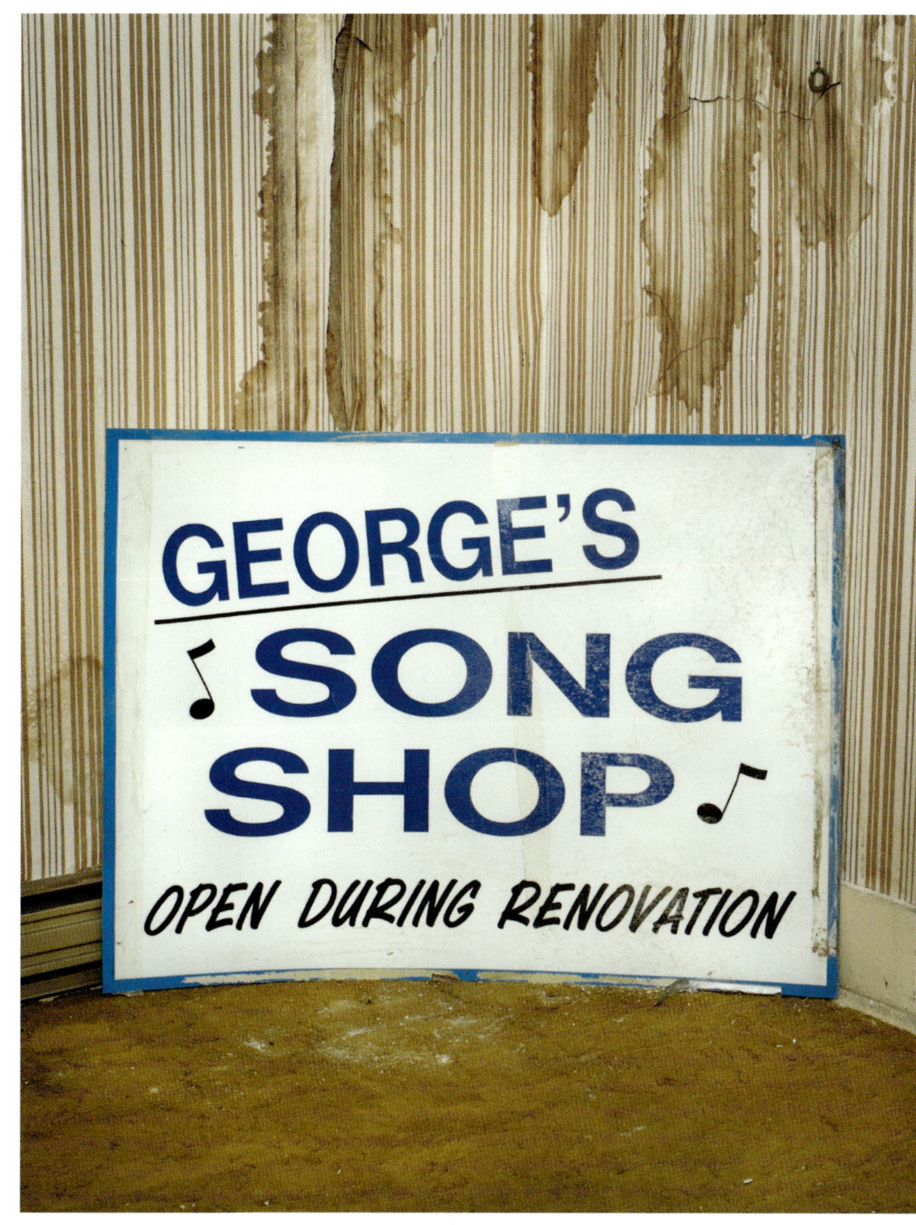

GEORGE'S
SONG
SHOP
OPEN DURING RENOVATION

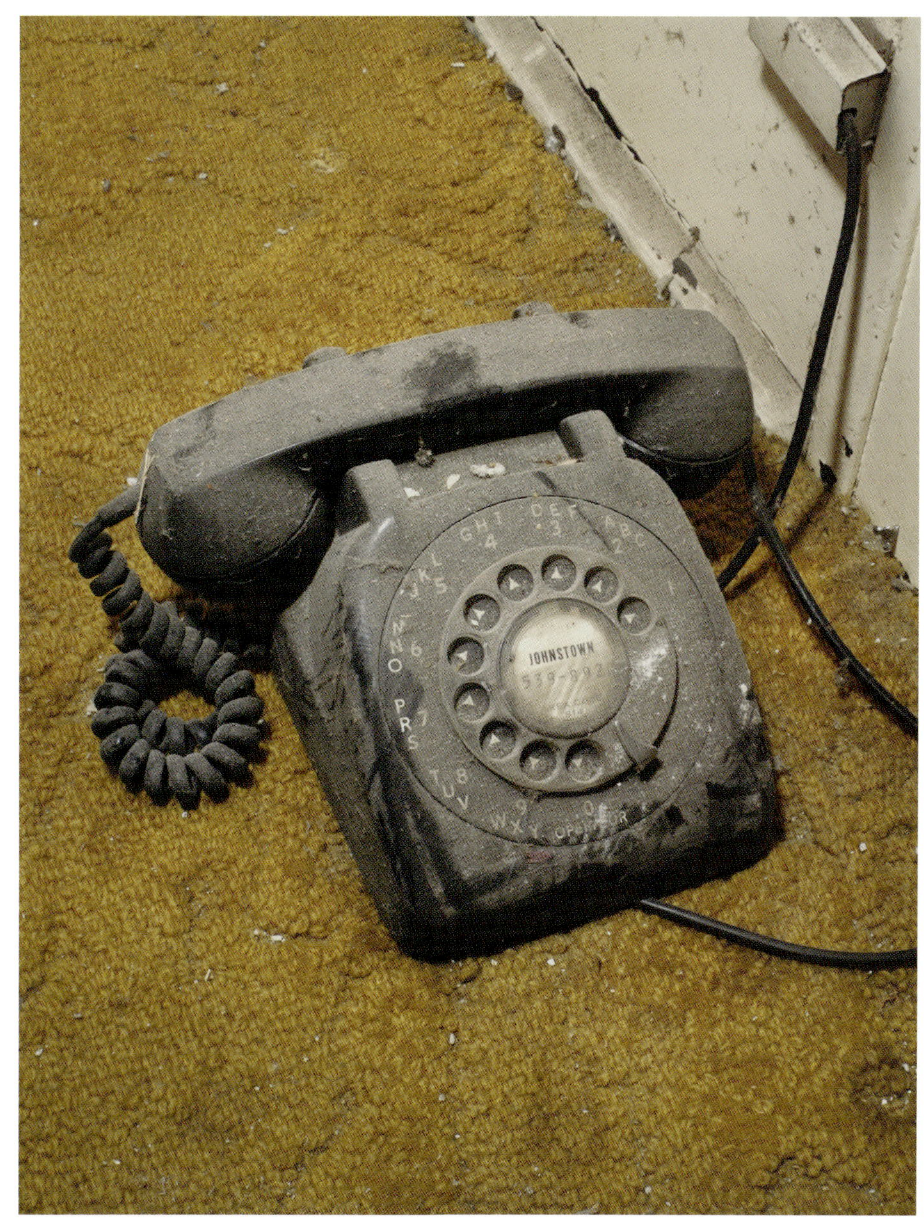

JOHNSTOWN
539-992

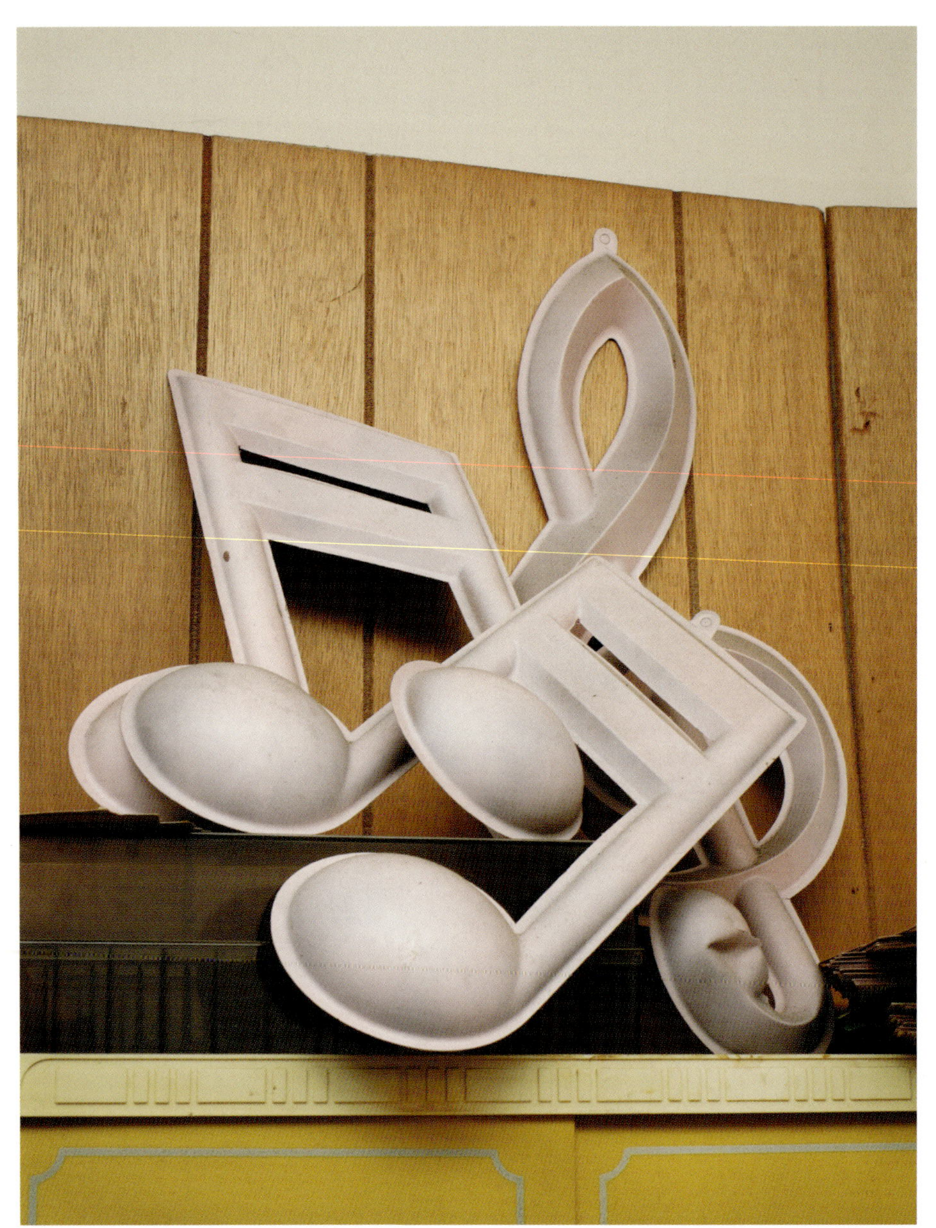

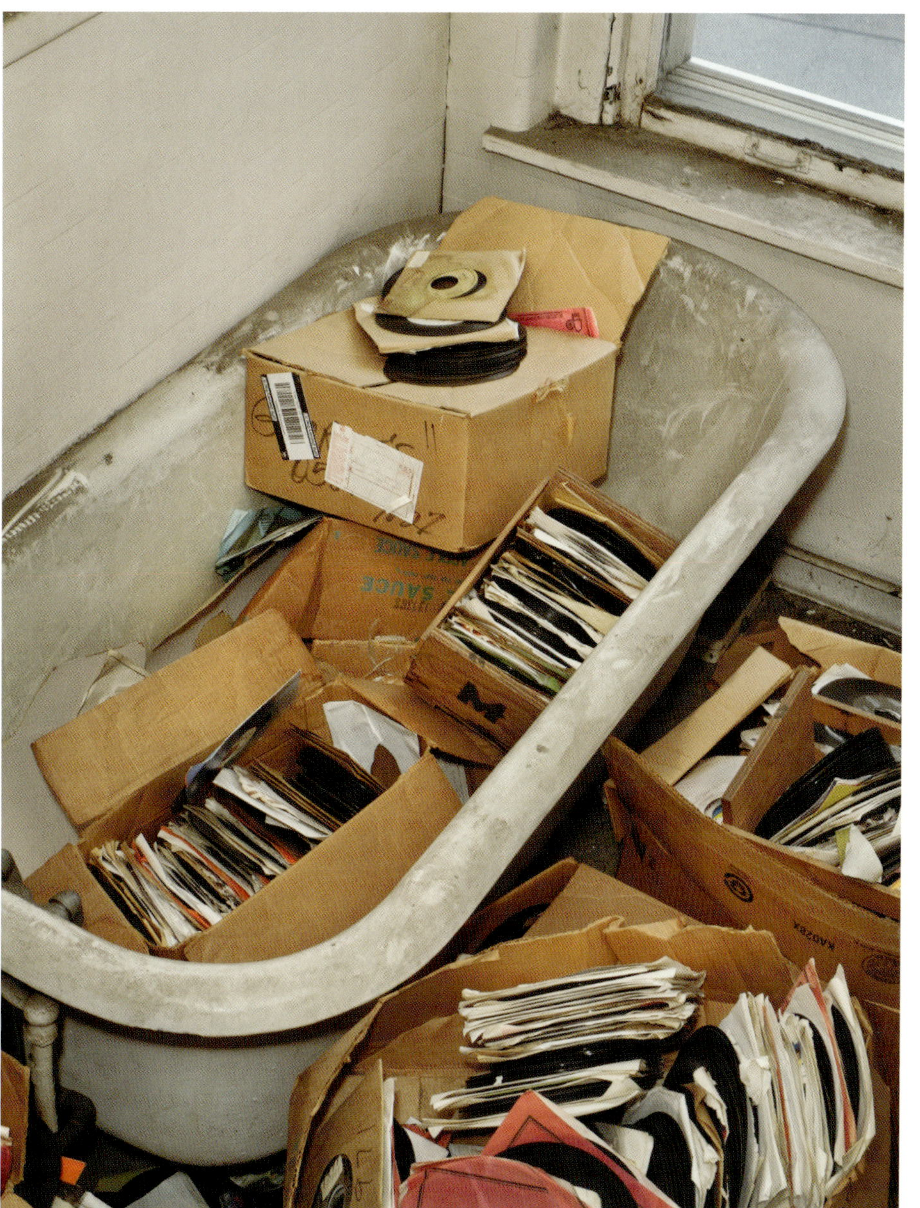

FIRST OF ALL, I ALWAYS SAID THIS.

I DON'T WANT TO GET EVERYTHING.

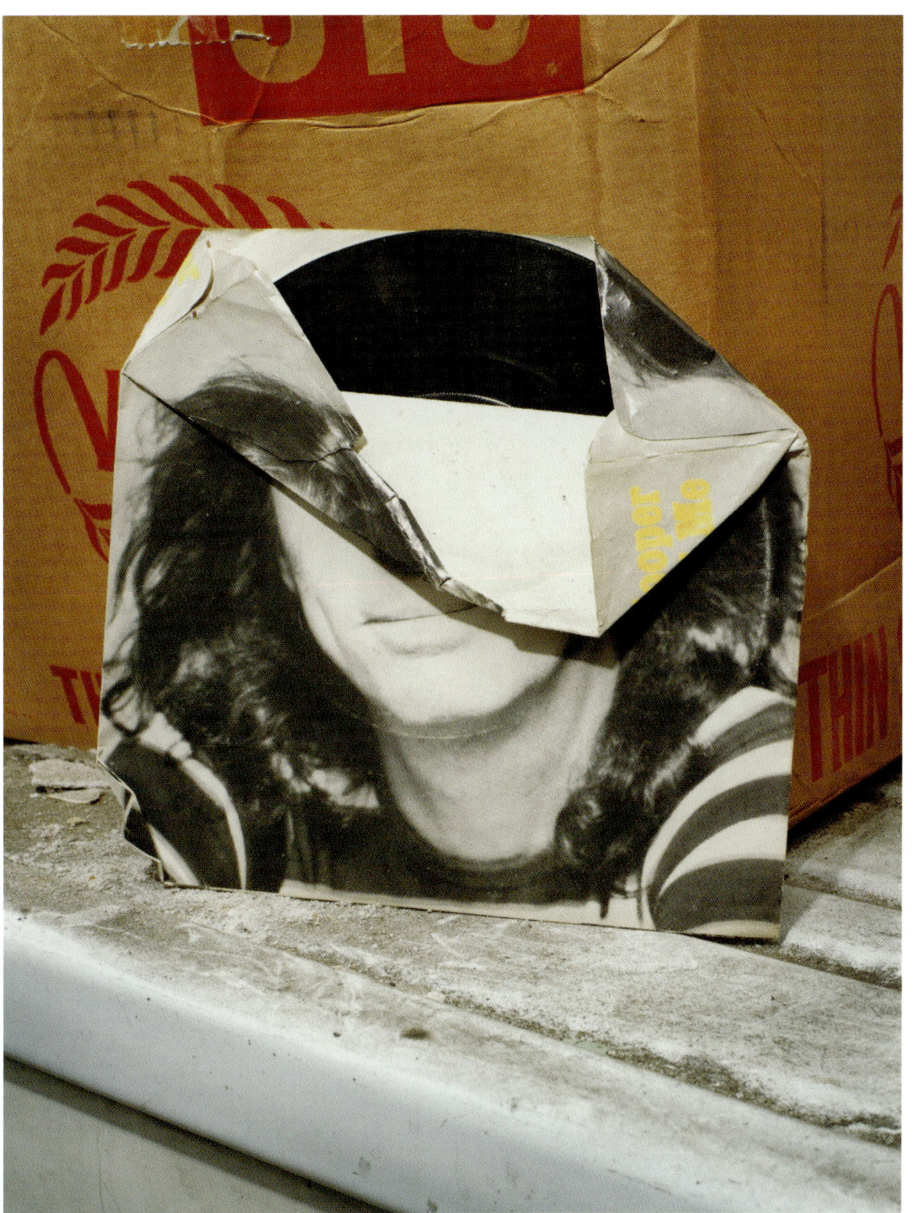
oper
Me
THIN

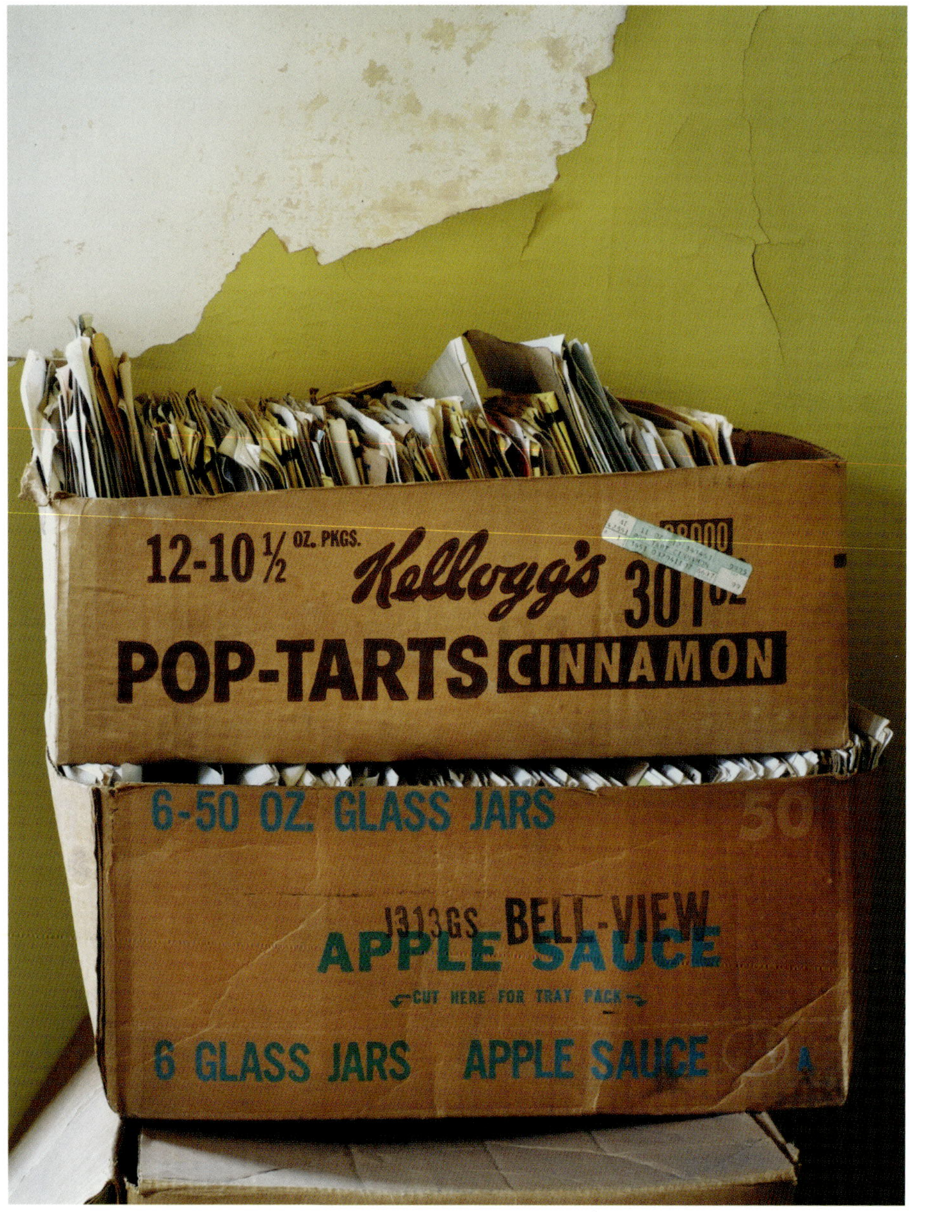
12-10 ½ OZ. PKGS.
Kellogg's 30 OZ
POP-TARTS CINNAMON
88000
6-50 OZ. GLASS JARS
50
J313GS BELL-VIEW
APPLE SAUCE
CUT HERE FOR TRAY PACK
6 GLASS JARS   APPLE SAUCE
A

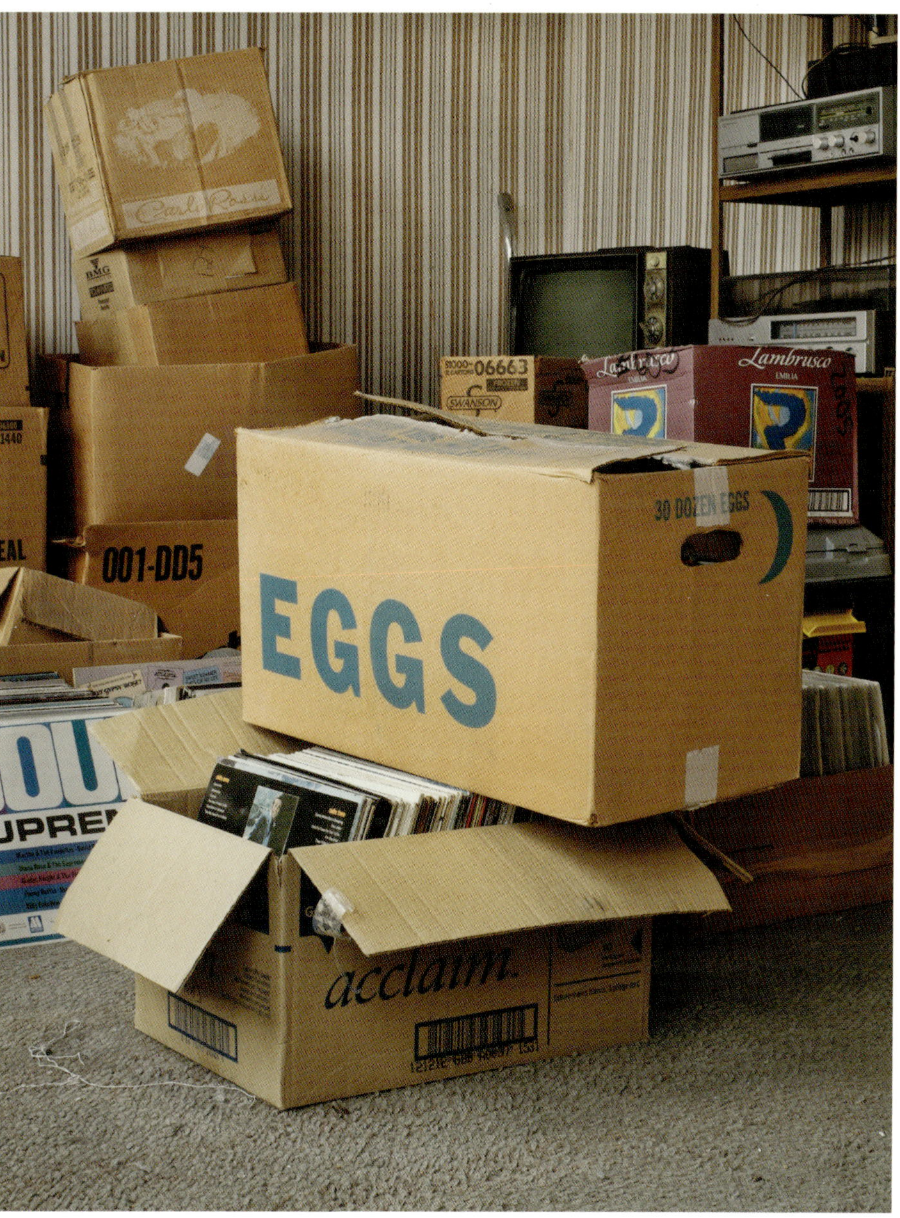
Carlo Rossi
BMG
001-DD5
EAL
30 DOZEN EGGS
EGGS
S1000- 06663
SWANSON
Lambrusco
Lambrusco
SUPRE
acclaim

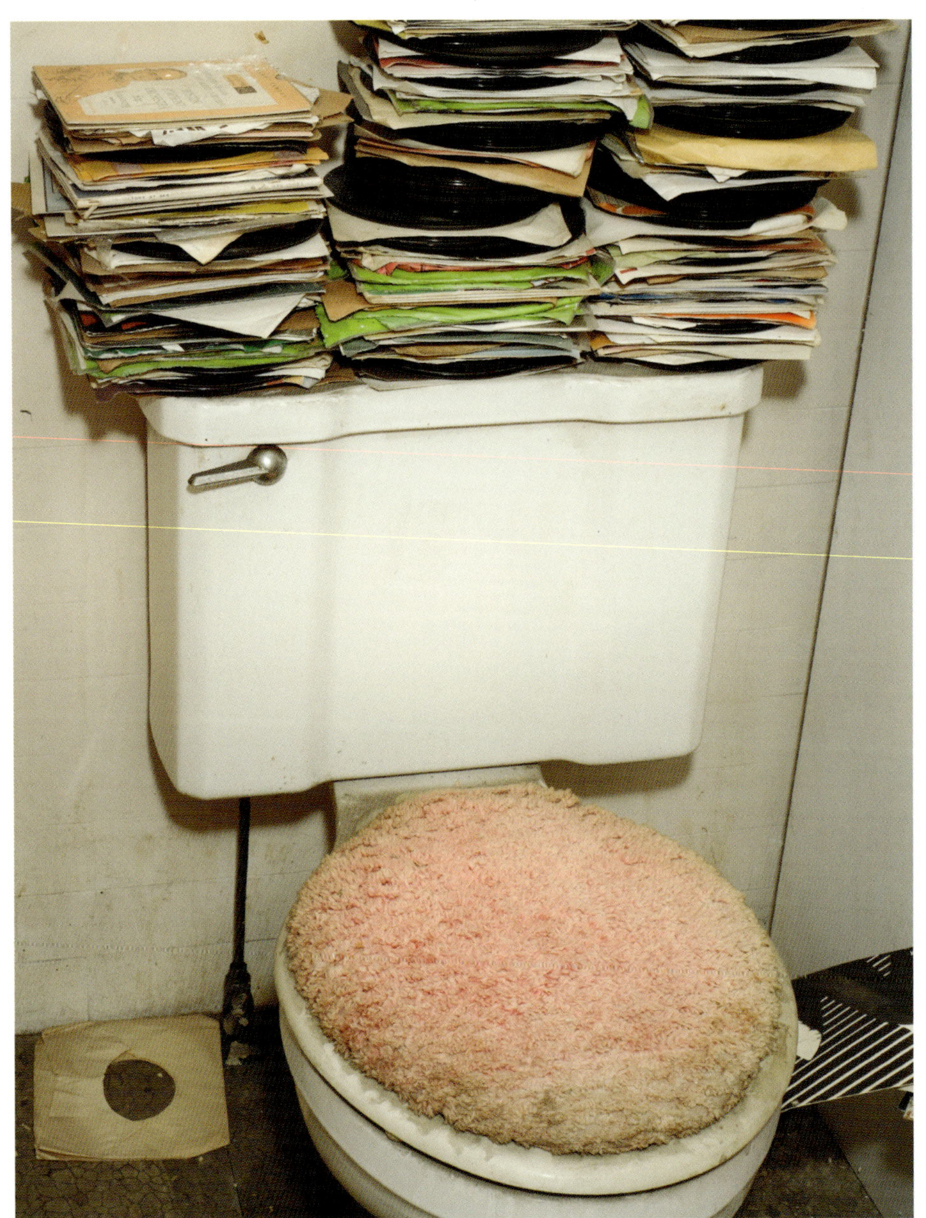

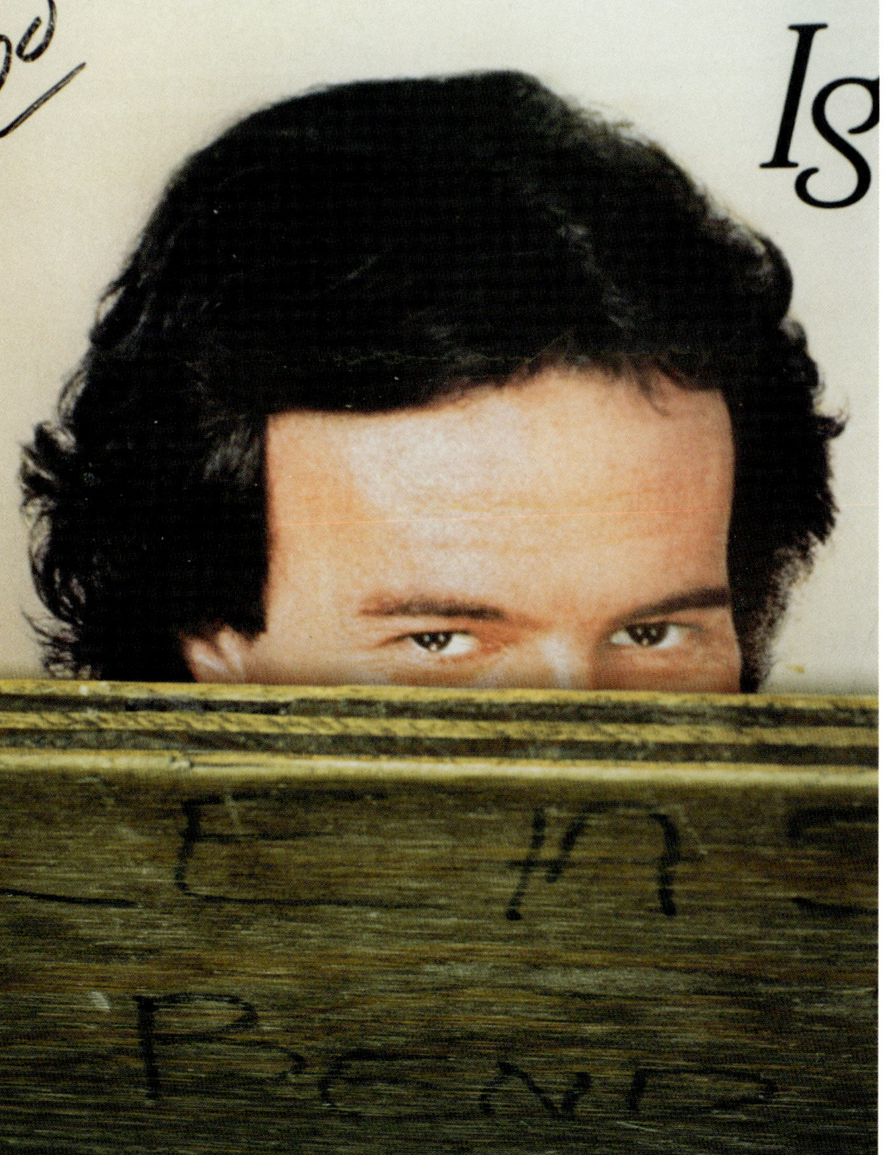
Is

AS MUCH AS I DO, I DON'T.

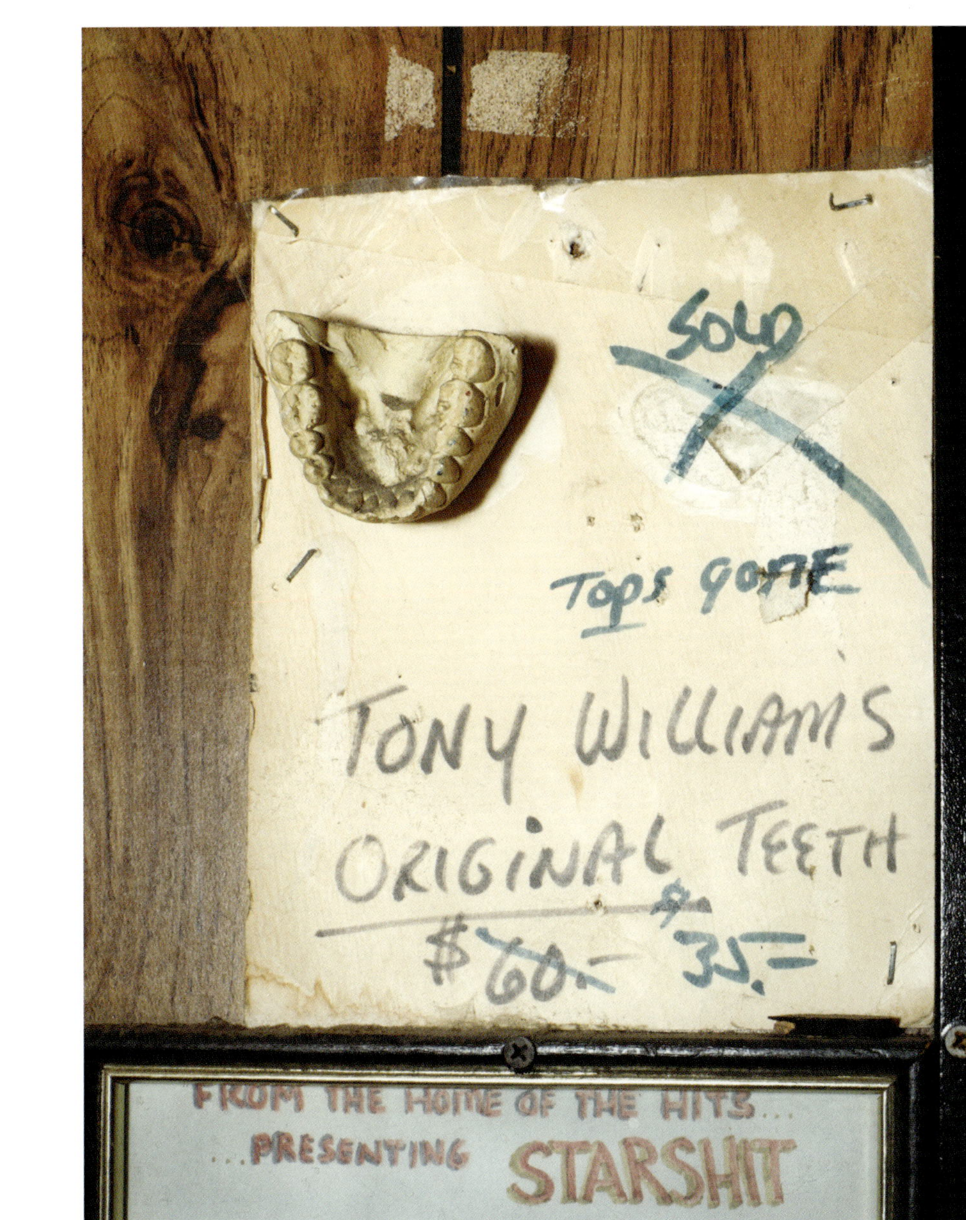
SOLD
Tops gone
TONY WILLIAMS
ORIGINAL TEETH
$60.- 35.-
FROM THE HOME OF THE HITS...
...PRESENTING STARSHIT

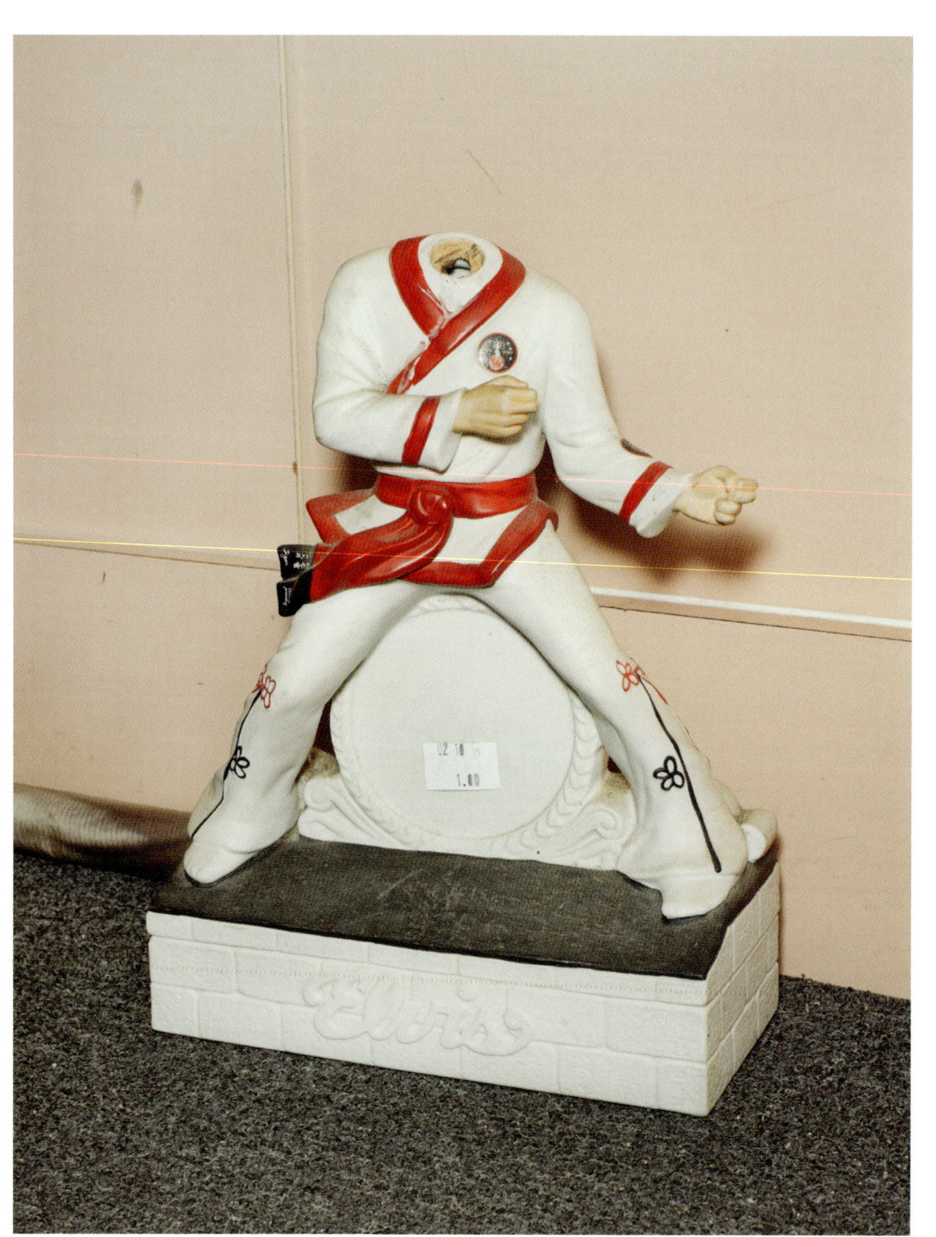

Elvis

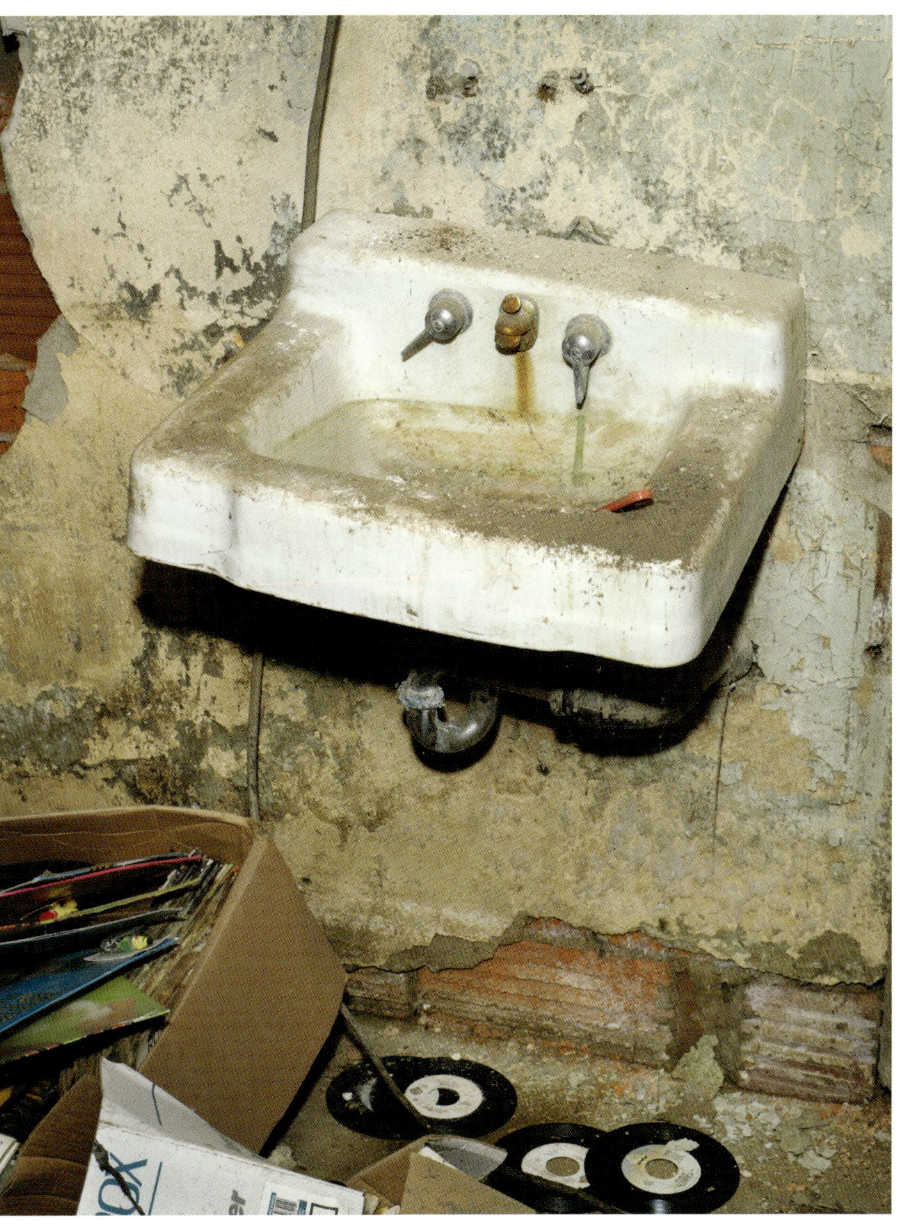

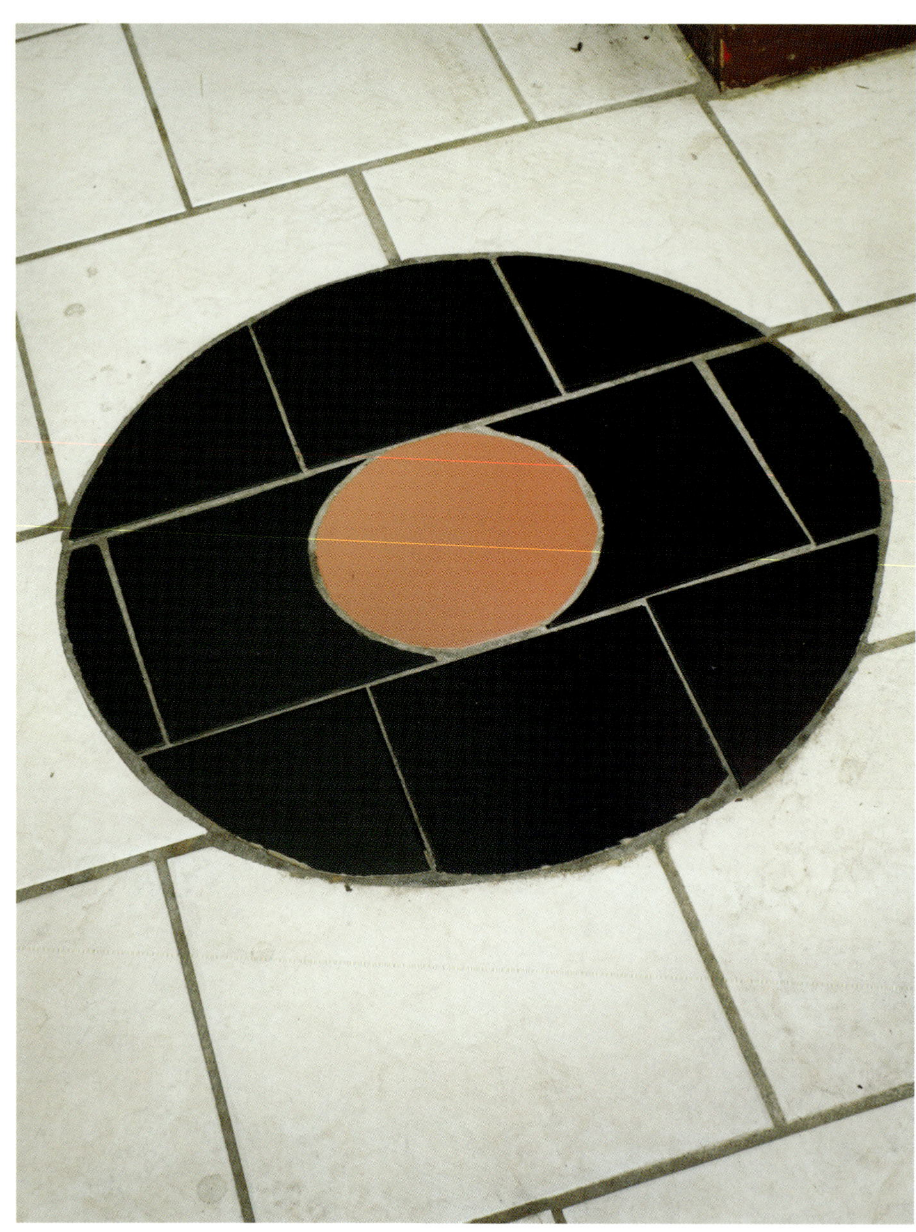

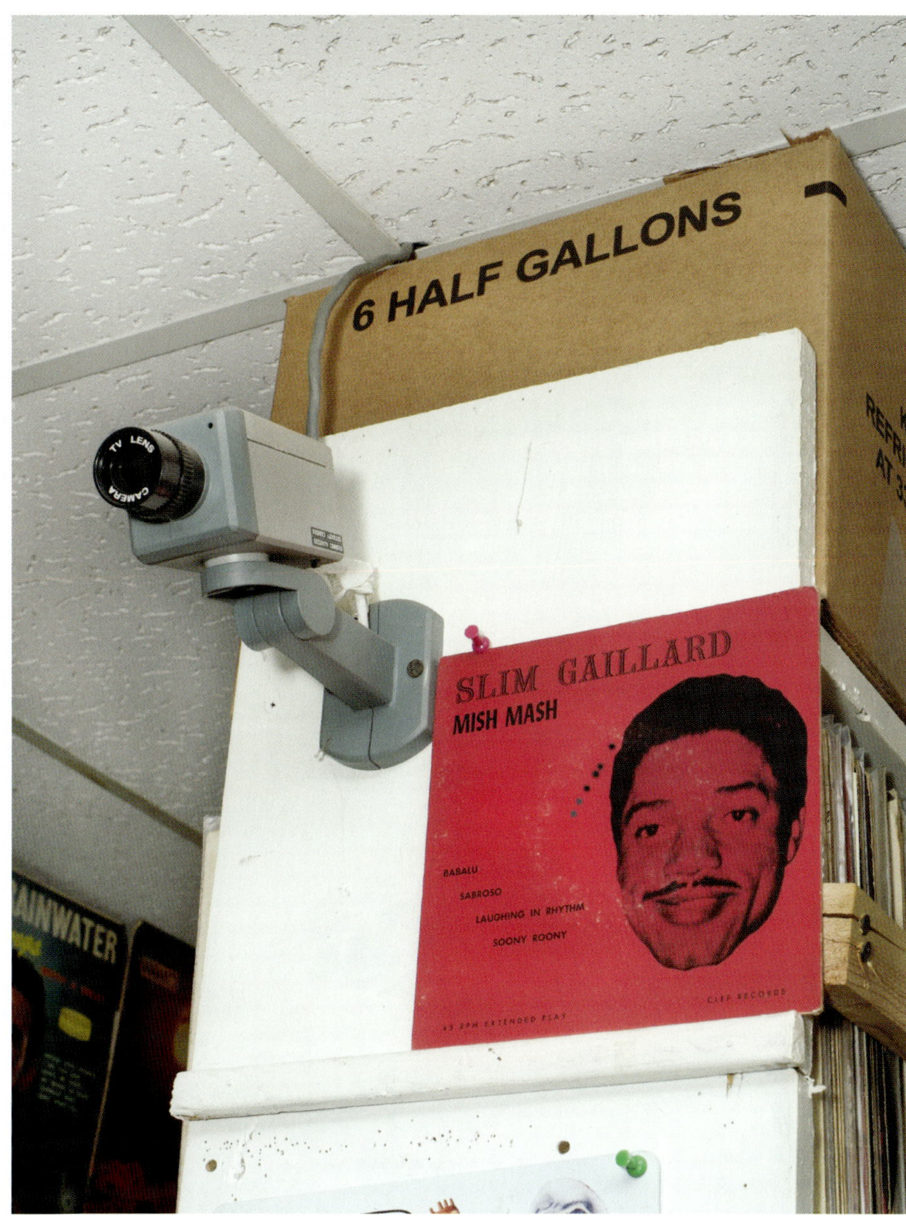
6 HALF GALLONS
TV LENS
CAMERA
SLIM GAILLARD
MISH MASH
BABALU
SABROSO
LAUGHING IN RHYTHM
SOONY ROONY
45 RPM EXTENDED PLAY
RAINWATER

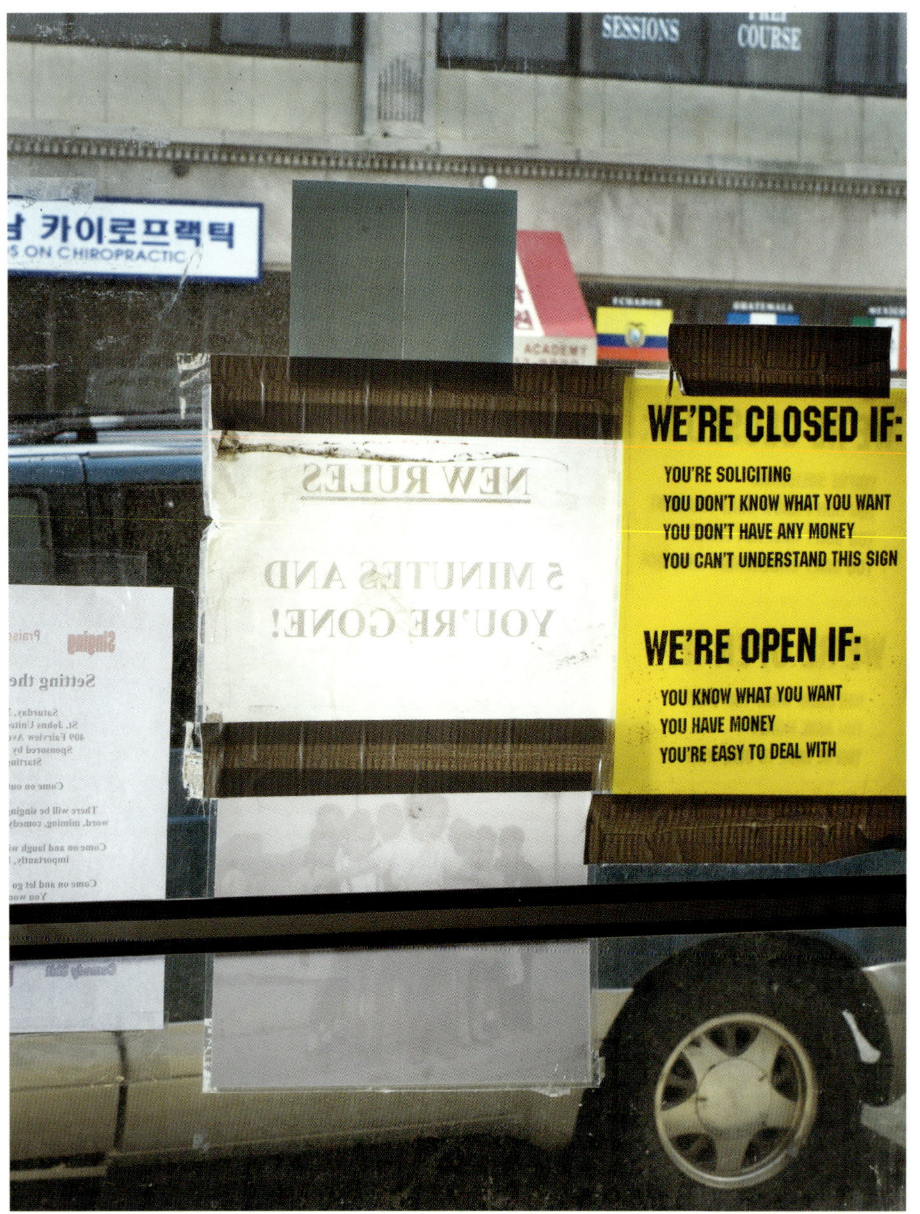
SESSIONS
FREE
COURSE
카이로프랙틱
S ON CHIROPRACTIC
ACADEMY
ECUADOR
GUATEMALA
NEW RULES
5 MINUTES AND
YOU'RE GONE!
WE'RE CLOSED IF:
YOU'RE SOLICITING
YOU DON'T KNOW WHAT YOU WANT
YOU DON'T HAVE ANY MONEY
YOU CAN'T UNDERSTAND THIS SIGN
WE'RE OPEN IF:
YOU KNOW WHAT YOU WANT
YOU HAVE MONEY
YOU'RE EASY TO DEAL WITH
Singing
Praise
Setting the

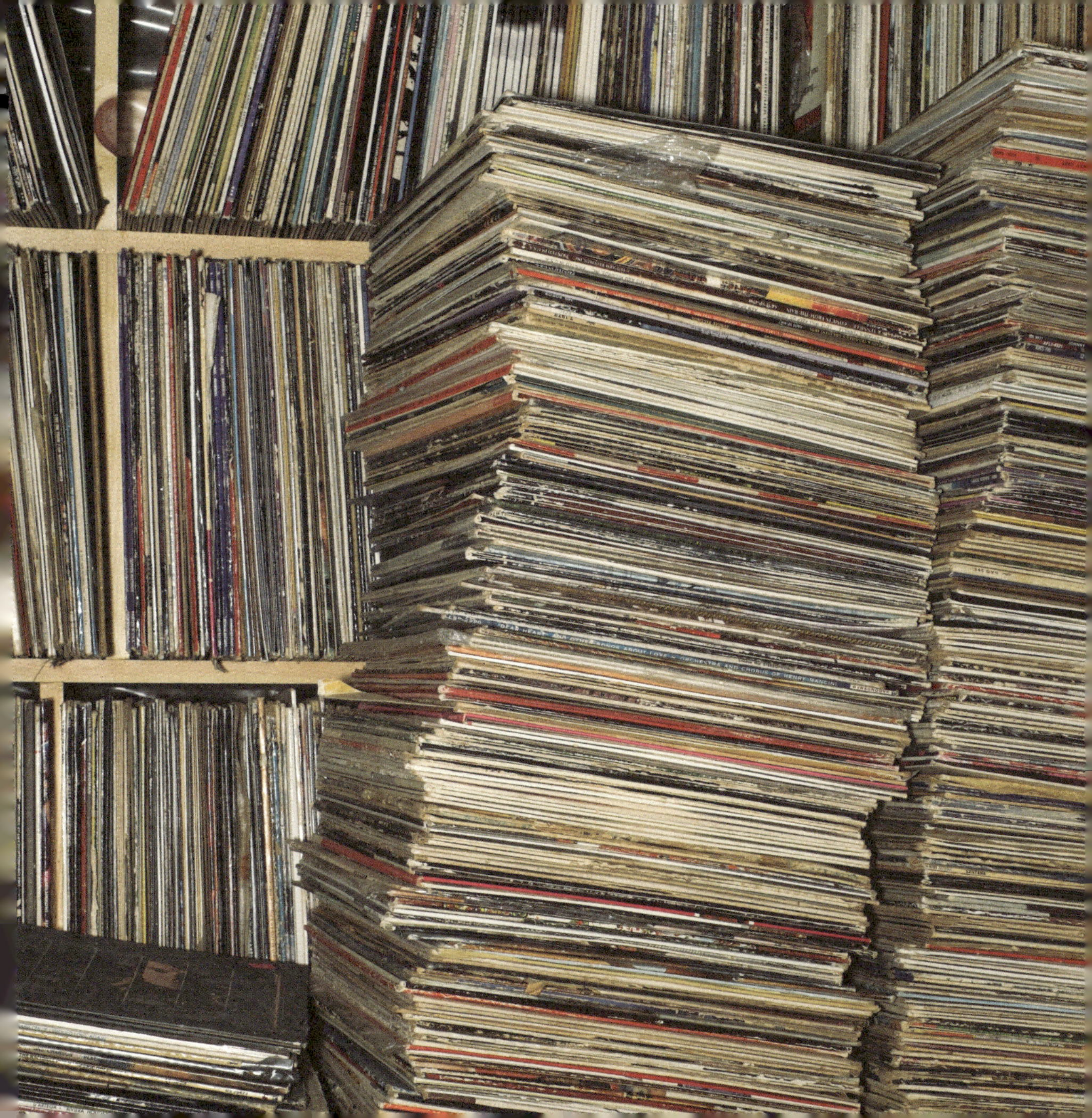

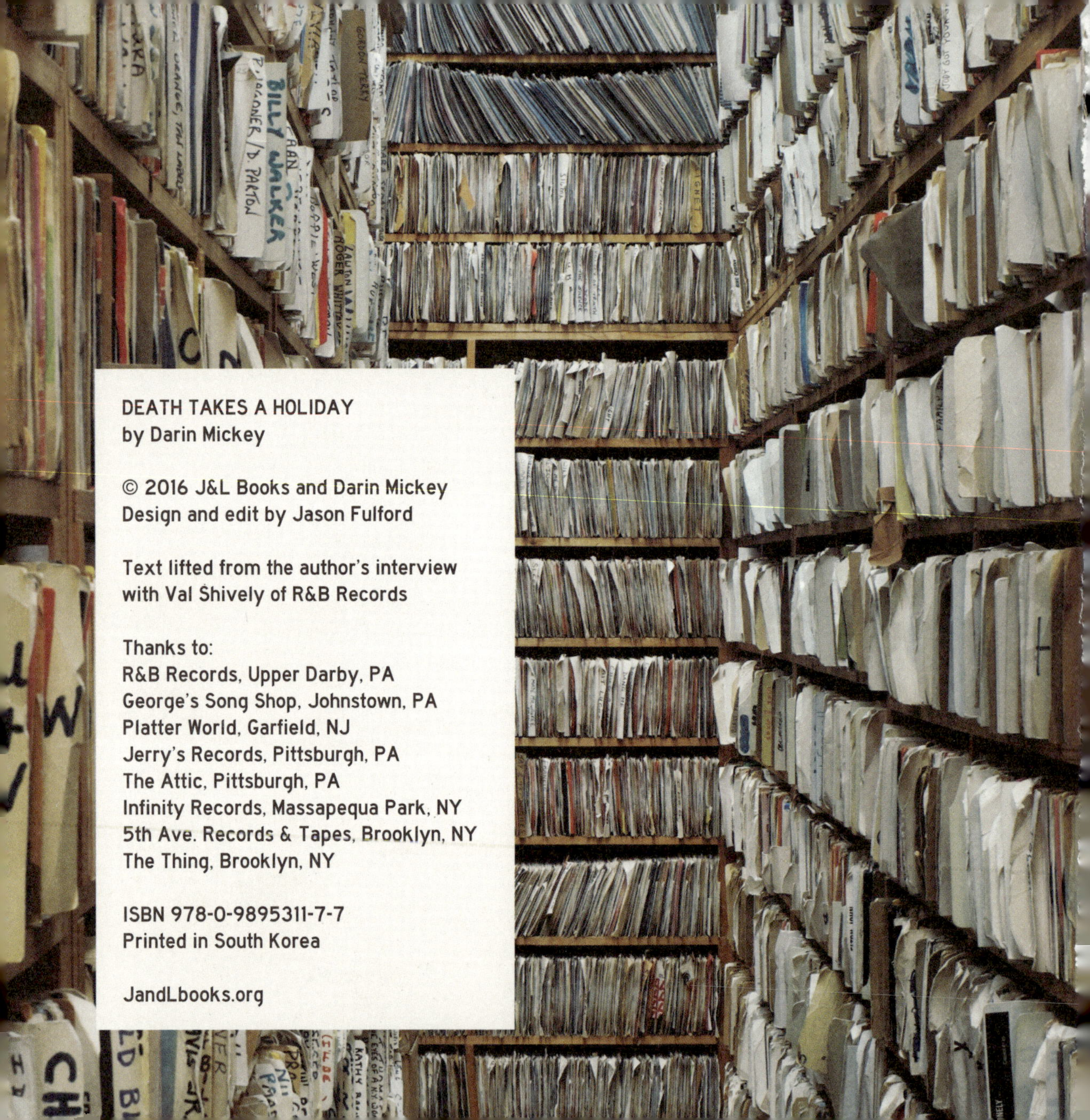

DEATH TAKES A HOLIDAY
by Darin Mickey

© 2016 J&L Books and Darin Mickey
Design and edit by Jason Fulford

Text lifted from the author's interview
with Val Shively of R&B Records

Thanks to:
R&B Records, Upper Darby, PA
George's Song Shop, Johnstown, PA
Platter World, Garfield, NJ
Jerry's Records, Pittsburgh, PA
The Attic, Pittsburgh, PA
Infinity Records, Massapequa Park, NY
5th Ave. Records & Tapes, Brooklyn, NY
The Thing, Brooklyn, NY

ISBN 978-0-9895311-7-7
Printed in South Korea

JandLbooks.org